The Power of OPE

The Power of OPE

The Key to Exponential Growth is Embracing Other People's Everything

Bethany LaFlam

Published by Game Changer Publishing

Cover Design: Skylar Cawley

Paperback ISBN: 978-1-966659-28-0

Hardcover ISBN: 978-1-966659-29-7

Digital ISBN: 978-1-966659-30-3

GC GAME CHANGER
PUBLISHING
www.GameChangerPublishing.com

Dedication

To my very favorite OP, Mackenzie —

You are the spark that brought this book to life. Because of you,
I finally sought out my OPs—not just to build, but to be more present,
to savor life alongside you. You've taught me that life isn't meant to
be a constant chase toward some distant goal but a dance
in the moment, filled with joy and magic.

My deepest wish for you is this: to fully embrace
the Power of OPE in every pursuit, to know that you are
the creator of your extraordinary life, and to always BE
the truest, most beautiful version of yourself—
which to me, is absolute perfection.

Read This First

Just to say thanks for buying and reading my book,
I would like to give you a *free* gift,
no strings attached.

SCAN ME

The Power of OPE

The Key to Exponential Growth is Embracing
Other People's Everything

Bethany LaFlam

Foreword

When Bethany LaFlam first introduced me to the concept of *Other People's Everything* (OPE), I thought I understood leverage. As a seasoned real estate investor and entrepreneur, I've built businesses by surrounding myself with the right people. But what Bethany has created with *The Power of OPE* goes far beyond what most of us recognize as delegation or teamwork—it's a whole new lens through which to view growth, success, and freedom.

Bethany has lived the lessons in this book. I've had the privilege of watching her not only build her own empire but empower countless entrepreneurs—including myself—to break free from burnout, scale sustainably, and rediscover the joy of creating wealth. She's a master at spotting hidden potential, not just in deals but in people. Her superpower isn't just teaching strategy; it's unlocking possibility in everyone she meets.

The first time we worked together, I was struck by how Bethany approaches business with equal parts heart and precision. She believes that wealth, when created consciously, can transform lives far beyond our own. And in this book, she lays out the roadmap for doing exactly that—using OPE to magnify not only financial returns but the kind of abundance that makes life worth living.

The Power of OPE isn't just about building a successful business; it's about creating a life of freedom, impact, and joy. It's about learning to let go of the grind and embrace the opportunities that come from aligning with the right people.

If you're ready to stop hustling and start scaling—to work smarter, not harder—then you're holding the right book in your hands. Bethany's insights will shift the way you think about leadership, wealth, and what's truly possible when you stop trying to do it all alone.

I am honored to call Bethany a friend, a trusted advisor, and an inspiration. And I know that by the time you finish this book, you'll feel the same.

–*Ashley Wilson*
Entrepreneur, Author, and Real Estate Investor

Contents

Introduction

When I was young, I thought being driven, ambitious, and audacious were the most important things I could be. So I was. I toiled, and I wore my work ethic, fatigue, long hours, and struggle like a badge of honor. I thought having a more harrowing story would somehow later be traded for a spot in some eternal bliss where one was valued for pedaling faster and harder than the next guy. Even if that were true, SO WHAT? I worked harder than everyone so I could be lauded WHEN I WAS DEAD? Hard pass. I did attain some level of success by sheer brute force, sure. But I was not my best self, and I definitely was not healthy.

When I had my daughter, Mackenzie, that level of work would have meant that I had to sacrifice time with her in order to be successful. Again, hard pass. I wanted it all. I wanted success in business *and* to be a present and devoted mama. I'll admit, it wasn't immediate. For years, I felt like I was neither the best mom nor as successful as I knew I could or should be, and I also felt like I just had no more to give. It wasn't until I really started to focus inward and see how I was impeding my own success that it started to dawn on me. And, funnily enough, it wasn't until I sought help from someone outside myself that I learned that I had everything I needed within myself to be whole and happy. That will make more sense as you read on.

I thought I could educate my way around my mindset. I thought formal education could replace my self-doubt and my scarcity mindset (not that I had those words for it back then). I thought becoming a lawyer would let me graduate from my old life into a new life. And it elevated me to an extent. I am not saying don't get educated. I am saying it can take you only so far. Your mindset is what will take you where you need to be. And while you do have everything you need within you to build a magical life, sometimes you must recognize you need other people to help you. And other people need you to help them. It's a beautiful arrangement. If you surround yourself with the right WHOs (see *Who Not How* by Dan Sullivan and Dr. Benjamin Hardy for more on this), then you can achieve infinitely more success and happiness by doing only that which you love and at which you excel and letting others do the same. Asking for help may be the single hardest thing I ever did. It was harder than being a lawyer. Harder than being a mother. Harder than being a business owner. Yet, as soon as I did, the change was exponential and swift, relatively speaking.

If you've been an entrepreneur for more than five minutes, you have surely heard about the concept of Other People's Money (OPM). The proverbial "they" say that the way to get truly rich is to use OPM. I agree. Mostly. Taking that to its next logical step, because being rich is not the sole answer to being happy and living your heart's desire, is that you need to use OPE (Other People's EVERYTHING) to truly live your best life. Let me explain.

What I have come to know as my "heart-mind" has become my driving force for being the creator of my life. My own conjuror of joy. If you know me in real life (IRL), then you know that those words are not mine. (See? OPE.) One of my coaches (actually, she prefers "mindset strategist"), Susan, really taught me to receive.

"To be open to receiving," she said, "you have to not always be in your head."

I said, "OK, Susan. But my brain lives in my head, and she makes all the decisions around here."

She gently pointed out that living in my head all the time left me exhausted and unsatisfied. Fair point. She got me to look inward to let me really feel what it is that I wanted. Not think it, feel it. To do that, you have to let your heart in on the conversation. Turns out, that's where my inner goddess likes to hang out. She was like, "Finally, jeez." The inner goddess, I mean, not Susan. Susan was much more patient with me. And that was the beginning of how I started to create the shifts that started creating change in my life. Exponential change.

I took the leap and joined her entry-level mastermind group. I still had some mindset shit to sort out before I got to the big leagues. It was the most money I had ever spent on myself where I did not know the specific thing I was supposed to get out of it. Botox and fillers were clear to me, but this? These things are not transactional, and it was really uncomfortable to spend that much money on something intangible when part of what I needed was to make more money. At first, I showed up with a kind of "doesn't everyone know how busy I am" attitude, almost angry at myself for not only spending the money but also committing so much time to something that was not billable or actively building my business. It was the best investment I ever made. *You* are your best investment. Every. Damn. Time. I learned so much about myself, not only from Susan facilitating the group but from the other members sharing as well.

Once I started really taking advantage of the mastermind, including finally scheduling and showing up to my one-on-one sessions where I got to dive deep into my limiting beliefs, I had a major shift. It was like a drug. I wanted more of the feel-good, and I wanted to set and achieve the next goal and share my big brag (we brag in our masterminds, and if you don't, you should), and I wanted to hear about the epic things others in my group were doing. I started to have so much fun envisioning my huge future. I had more time freedom. I was making more money. I was a better business owner, lawyer, and mother because I was feeding my soul and not punishing myself for not toiling for the sake of toiling.

Fairly quickly, I graduated to Ascension Wealth Consciousness, and my mindset had shifted such that I gladly paid the money, this time more than double what I had paid before, and I scheduled my life around the sessions. I even curated my very own mastermind within Ascension, so I could stack my deck and surround myself with people who would help get me to my magical life and whom I could help get to theirs. A lot of what is in this book was born in my mastermind sessions. I continue to consume all manner of self-help content, although I would like to submit a formal request to change the name of the genre.

OPE is really more of a compilation of ideas and lessons I have learned over my lifetime and really only recently began to put into practice through my own filter and as seen through my lens, which seems to get clearer the more I learn and the more I share. I am practicing the principles in this book, which are to take the pieces I need from the experts, give the pieces I have where I am the expert, and create a magical life with the whole, which, as the saying goes, is greater than the sum of those pieces.

We are often taught we should not use anything from other people for our own gain. The directive has been to keep your eyes on your own paper and whatnot. And I am certainly not advocating stealing another's work or intellectual property without giving proper credit, making it your own, or paying for it. What I am advocating is that you look inward and determine what your unique gifts and talents are, what you both excel at and love, and honor that. Likewise, when you encounter others that you admire, respect, and trust, recognize their unique gifts and talents and honor that. Then y'all stay in your lane and out of each other's way! OK, so what do I even mean when I say OPE?

Well, first off, I cannot say OPE without thinking of Naughty By Nature and singing "O.P.P." in my head. Every. Damn. Time. The first two letters are the same, but the last is something different. By the end of this book, you too will be down with OPE. Good luck getting it out of your head now. The E is for everything. The whole Universe is available to you as a resource. Think you can't achieve something amazing and epic? If you have thought of it, it is already done. Your job now is to search out what you need to make it real right now. This book is meant to be a starting place for how you can build your empire by bringing to the table your gifts and talents and then collaborating, borrowing, or leveraging everything else.

Chapter 1
The Keys to Exponential Growth

Exponential is one of those words that is just magical to me. Like limitless, exponential growth is a powerful concept that can help your business reach new heights. It occurs when a quantity grows at an increasing rate, meaning that the growth rate itself grows over time. In simpler terms, it's the idea that if you double something repeatedly, it will grow much faster than if you increase it by a fixed amount each time.

For example, if you start with one penny and double it every day for 30 days, you will end up with more than $5 million. Don't believe me? Let me save you a ChatGPT search: $.01 \times 2^{29} = \$5,368,709.12$. That's the power of exponential growth! Be honest; as an entrepreneur, nothing ever moves fast enough for you. So, why would you ever settle for anything *but* exponential growth?

How can you harness this power for your business? Exponential growth is a phenomenon that has been studied and utilized by businesses for many years. It is a powerful tool that can help companies achieve rapid growth and success, but it must be managed carefully to avoid negative consequences. Whatever you feed it, your constant will grow exponentially, for better or worse.

So, if you aren't intentional here, we can have a cancerous growth that can get out of control quickly.

Exponential growth in business is a type of growth that occurs when a company's revenue, profits, or market share grows at an increasing rate over time. This growth is often driven by factors such as innovation, market demand, and economies of scale. Companies that experience exponential growth can quickly become dominant players in their industries and achieve high levels of success. Great, but how? Well, there are the obvious answers you've heard over and over: innovation, scalability, marketing and sales, partnerships and alliances, and data and analytics. All true, of course. Companies that innovate and develop new products or services to meet the needs of their customers can experience rapid growth. By continuously innovating and staying ahead of the competition, companies can expand their customer base and increase their market share. Companies that scale their operations quickly and efficiently can take advantage of economies of scale and achieve exponential growth. This may involve investing in technology, hiring additional staff, or expanding into new markets. Companies that have effective marketing and sales strategies can attract new customers and increase revenue. By investing in marketing and sales, companies can create a strong brand image and build a loyal customer base. Companies that form strategic partnerships and alliances with other businesses can access new markets, technologies, and resources that can fuel exponential growth. Companies that use data and analytics to inform their decision-making can identify opportunities for growth and optimize their operations. By using data to track customer behavior, market trends, and other key metrics, companies can make informed decisions that drive exponential growth.

Those concepts are certainly required for exponential growth. But simply listing them fails to explain how this happens. Hate to disappoint you, but I won't go into a long, drawn-out chapter on it either. I won't do that because you don't need to know that. You need to know the "who" for each of those things if they are not squarely within your lane. Your Other People (OP) will work with you to take each of these concepts through to reality. If they are the right OPs, you will all have fun doing it, and it will happen much faster than you trying to figure it all out on your own—the results will be astounding. I promise.

While exponential growth is the goal of most entrepreneurs, it can also lead to challenges and risks that must be managed carefully. Companies that experience exponential growth may need to invest heavily in new infrastructure, technology, and staff to support their operations. To manage this growth effectively, you must ensure you have adequate financial resources and a solid financial management plan in place. See Chapter 4 on Other People's Money if you need guidance here.

As your company grows, you must adapt your organizational structure to ensure you can continue to operate efficiently and effectively. This may involve hiring new staff, creating new departments, or restructuring existing ones. Exponential growth can also create new risks for businesses, such as market saturation, increased competition, or supply chain disruptions. To manage these risks, you must develop robust risk management strategies and contingency plans.

Please be intentional about your growth. You have a vision, and that likely includes what you want the customer experience to be. Don't lose sight of that for the sake of growth, or you risk reaching the pinnacle and hating the view.

What Is B to the Power of E?

My company name is B to the Power of E, and it has deep and profound meaning to me, so I want to share it with you. So, what does B to the Power of E even mean, and why is it important? Well, first, it is a reminder to just BE. You don't always have to DO or THINK or PERFORM or ACHIEVE. These things will happen naturally if you focus on just BEing. Be present with yourself, with your loved ones, with your mind and body. B to the Power of E, or $B^{(e)}$ also has significance in science and math as it relates to physical and economic phenomena. The letter "e" is used in many mathematical calculations for the exponential constant. I have turned that on its head and made "B" the constant and "e" the exponent. When *you* are constant, when you can allow yourself to just BE, then you can create exponential growth. Just as in math, as the "e" grows, the value of "B," which is the value of you, is limitless. So what is the "e" if "B" is the constant? The exponent can have any value, and the greater the value, the more exponential growth you will achieve. The "e" is the EVERYTHING you are feeding the "B." It includes your environment, the Other People with whom you associate, and what you consume in the way of books and social media. So, choose wisely, because there is also a negative exponential function.

B to the Power of E also stands for building your empire. Nobody can build an empire completely on their own. I have several mentors, coaches, mindset strategists, and Other People working with me. My B to the Power of E retreats, for example, feature a mindset and mindfulness component, along with the framework to figure out where you need support and the means to get it. The power of proximity means you get to increase the number of positive connections in your life and surround yourself with support and other empire builders. In this book, I will focus on how to BE the strongest B, or constant, you can be, what of Other People's things cause a negative exponential function, and what of Other People's things can exponentially increase your ability to live a truly magical existence.

Being Your Own Constant

In the journey toward conscious wealth and empire building, there exists a potent source of power that many overlook or underestimate—the power of Other People's Everything (OPE). The power of OPE is that it allows you to focus on making yourself the very best you can be and honing your unique gifts and talents while allowing your Other People to contribute theirs. Using OPE does *not* mean you can neglect your SELF. You have to be your own constant, or the E won't add much value. Zero to the power of anything is still zero. You need to invest in yourself. You need to have a solid foundation not just in your financial self but in your health, your community/relationships, and your connection to spirituality or your highest self. However you frame your connection, it is something bigger than yourself. Neglecting any one of these will negatively impact the value of your constant that provides the base for your exponential growth.

Do What You Love

Truly knowing yourself is also essential for growth. When your self-knowledge is elevated, you can open up to Other People and businesses and build meaningful relationships with them. Identifying and then eliminating your limiting beliefs is one critical step in this process. Another is to identify and strengthen your unique gifts and talents. If you know what you truly love to do and what you excel at, and you truly believe you can live your life in your heart's desire by staying in your lane (aka performing your unique superpower), then you will have limitless inspiration. (There's that word again: *limitless.* Is there a better word than that?) From there, you can easily learn how you can change your mental and physical state in your next breath. Your base, your constant, then provides the best possible foundation for *everything* to enjoy exponential growth.

I did a branding exercise a while back as a result of having completed a hardcore visioning exercise wherein I laid out what my empire looks like—my magical life. At the top, I have self-perpetuating and self-sustaining freedom (freedom to, not freedom from; see *The Gap and the Gain* by Dan Sullivan and Dr. Benjamin Hardy for more on this concept). My mindset strategist and I determined that the brand really had to be reflective of me and my authentic self. I had to put myself out there and embrace all parts of me. There is no balance or separation between personal life and work life. There is just me. And for you, there is just you. Own it. Use it. Build upon it.

Up until this visioning session, I really believed that I could only be the serious Securities and Exchange Commission (SEC) lawyer behind a desk and toil away in order to earn the credibility and freedom to write my books, host my retreats, speak, and educate people on how to scale their businesses, their wealth, and their extraordinary life experiences. I also believed that to pursue my other interests, which could be labeled by some as more "woo woo," I would have to start another business. The two were never to cross. I would use my other side hustle to build up a following of people who would attend retreats because hosting retreats at amazing properties that I own in beautiful locations around the world is my retirement plan. Getting paid to travel, have epic and unique experiences with incredible people, and build up my real estate portfolio at the same time is the dream.

The problem was I was so busy doing things I did not love that did not propel me closer to the top of my ultimate vision, and frankly, I kind of sucked at doing them. I was exhausted and cranky and not getting where I wanted to go fast enough. Why? Because I had not defined what my unique gifts and talents were or decided what "staying in my lane" really meant. I was doing everything, and none of it particularly efficiently. I was in that entrepreneurial trap of thinking if I just did everything myself, I could control the process and the outcome better than if I had to rely on Other People. I was in everyone's lane all at once.

> *"When you try to be everything to everyone,*
> *you accomplish being nothing to anyone."*
> –Bonnie Gillespie

Have you ever driven on a freeway and noticed the bumps on the side of the road? These bumps, also known as rumble strips, are designed to alert drivers when they are veering out of their lane. Staying in your lane means not only focusing on your own business and not getting distracted by what your competitors are doing; it also means staying true to your own vision and goals. When you stay in your own lane, you can stay focused on what you do best and what you love most. Your continued work on your *self* is a sort of rumble strip for you. You will learn to trust yourself to know when something is not meant for you. Or, your Other People will remind you.

Defining Your Lane

Imagine a competitive swimming pool with the red and blue lane dividers that force the swimmers to go in a semi-straight line down the length of the pool. When I swam in high school, I relied heavily on those lane lines to keep me from swerving over into another swimmer during backstroke. I would look at the ceiling tiles above me and swim close to the lines so I could sort of feel my way along. It was uncomfortable when I bumped into them, which happened when I wasn't hyper-focused on the strength and power of my kick and my stroke.

In hindsight, I was expending way too much energy even

hugging the lines. Just think about how much momentum I lost when I collided with them. I mean, the really good swimmers on my team (I was average at best) swam straight down the middle, focused only right in front of them and on their breath. Their kicks and strokes had been practiced so much that they didn't need to think about it. They *knew* it. Their bodies and their minds had the knowledge of what to do embedded within them. They were centered. Our coach, Nathan Dockter (I can still smell his Drakkar Noir cologne, which gives you a little hint as to how old I am), guided us through meditations before big meets to get our mindset where it needed to be. That was my first experience with meditation, and I wish I could tell you I had developed a daily practice from that moment on, but it took me quite a few years to adopt a solid meditation practice. Before one particular meet, my last swim meet ever during my senior year of high school, the meditation really spoke to me. Something clicked like it never had before. I knew I had been holding back for some reason. I knew I had more in me to give. I didn't yet possess the tools and insights I now have to realize it was the fear of "what if I try my best and still fail" that was holding me back. So for three years I swam, giving it partial effort and accepting mediocre results.

Coach Nate said I was a natural the first time he saw me swim backstroke, but I didn't have the confidence to believe him. Somehow, though, his guided meditation the night before my very last swim meet shook something loose in me. And maybe it was partially that it was my last meet ever, so I had only one more shot, but whatever it was, I focused on my breath, and I unleashed everything I had the next day. He had taught me a better start, but I had been timid about it. This time, I did it anyway, and it felt perfect. I swam straight down the middle. I kicked as hard as I could, which was harder than I ever had before. My turns were perfectly timed without me slowing down to count strokes or look back for the wall. I trusted myself. As I rounded the turn after the first 50 yards, I could see Coach Nate standing over the edge, screaming his ever-loving head off, waving, and cheering, "YES! YES! GO! GO!" That made me kick even harder. Breathe even steadier. Trust even more. I had this. I didn't look over at any other lanes to see where the other swimmers were. I was focused only on my lane. When I touched the wall after the 100 yards were behind me, and I looked up at Coach for his approving jump for joy, he motioned for me to look behind me. I had beaten everyone in my heat by a lot. (Had I tried like that and trusted like that before, I would have been placed in a faster heat and probably would have gotten an even better time, but that 100-yard swim was my fastest by nearly six seconds!)

Focusing on myself and what I knew I needed to do and staying squarely in my lane caused me to have the best race of my life. And I know it seems silly, but imagine if you were in a race and you decided to cover your 100 yards by swimming across the lanes, over the lane lines, trying to dodge other swimmers doing their races. You will still eventually cover 100 yards, but it will take much longer, it will be much harder on you, it will most certainly piss off everyone else trying to swim in those other lanes, and you will never win that way. The same is true in all aspects of your life. Staying in your lane allows you to get further with less effort and with better overall results.

What is Conscious Wealth?

I talk about conscious wealth creation quite a lot, and it's really important to me. Helping people create conscious wealth is a big part of my particular lane. To me, conscious wealth is a way of doing business that goes beyond simply maximizing profits. It involves creating wealth in a way that is aligned with my values and mission, and that takes into account the impact that my business has on all of its stakeholders, including clients, employees, partners, and the broader community. Conscious wealth creation involves creating value for all of us, rather than just focusing on the money. But it also means focusing on the money. I used to believe that doing it for the money was an uncivilized reason to be in business. It was like making money was reserved for bad people, or at least people who weren't me. I had that "Who do I think I am to want to be rich?" mindset. Can you relate? If you can, I hope this book is a turning point for you to get past that limiting belief once and for all. If you can't, good for you! You are one step closer to creating your extraordinary life.

Let me tell you a story I read about Wayne Gretzky. He was known as one of the GREATEST hockey players of all time. His secret weapon was that he didn't spend all of his time and energy skating up and down the ice for no reason. Instead, he STRATE-GICALLY predicted the placement of the puck. He'd hustle there, get in front of the puck, and do what he needed to. Then he'd dial it back and wait for the next time he needed to turn it up. Why do I share this story? It's important because it demonstrates that hustle is not the same as the hustle culture we were taught.

We should strategize the best way to use our energy instead of getting tired midway through the game and burning out. Work smarter. Wealth consciousness is created when we are intentional in all our actions. Our effort is expended on what really matters at the time it matters. And when it's not our turn to hustle, we let our Other People do their hustle.

True conscious wealth creation extends this philosophy into actionable practices. It's about integrating your values into every facet of your business, from stakeholder engagement and ethical decision-making to sustainability and social impact. By prioritizing purpose alongside profit, you create value not just for yourself, but for everyone involved. Measuring this progress—whether through stakeholder satisfaction, environmental footprint, or ethical business practices—ensures that your efforts continuously evolve, creating long-term value and meaningful change.

Shifting Your Mindset

The three elements to creating conscious wealth in any area are education, access to opportunities, and mindset. That's it. In this day and age, we all have access to education with the internet—maybe not formal education, but the education we need to learn how to invest or learn how to start and run a business. There is nothing we can't access online. That said, I am also a big proponent of investing in yourself and attending events in person to get all three elements at once. Access to opportunities—we can all find opportunities—they are all around us all the time. Is access always equal? Nope. Life isn't always fair. Sometimes the starting lines are not at the same place. So then what do you do? SHIFT YOUR MINDSET! The thing that separates those who create conscious wealth and those who never do is mindset. It really is that simple, I promise. And lawyers (almost) never make promises.

Of these three elements, the most overlooked is mindset, but it is equally important. Maybe the most important. Have you ever heard someone super successful speak about how everything is too hard, so why bother? Do you think Tony Robbins somehow thinks he doesn't deserve success? He knows in his very soul that he does, and he uses that infectious mindset to empower others. One of my superpowers is that I see opportunities where others don't, and I can hear someone's goals and dreams and formulate a strategy to turn that into scalable results. One of the tools I have at my disposal is my ability to provide guardrails to help real estate investors build and scale their empires. I do that by knowing the rules and then helping my clients build a strategy to meet their goals within those rules. I know where there is room to be creative, and I know where we need to be rigid. My most successful clients are the ones with the mindset that they can be successful *and* stay within those guardrails. That takes a tremendous amount of trust, not just in me but in THEMSELVES. If they think they need to skate in the gray to be successful, then they will be less successful. And we are talking BIG personalities here—visionaries, entrepreneurs—but there's a peacefulness to having those guardrails if you have the right mindset.

Now, I want you to think about what your unique gifts and talents are. You may already have a good idea, or maybe you have never explored it before. An easy starting point is to think about what you are currently paid to do. Do you love it? Are you paid well for it? If you suddenly had $10 million, would you still do it? When you fantasize about your dream life, your empire having been built, with all your Other People in place, what are you doing in that empire? Be honest with yourself here.

Most personal development programs and speakers focus on tough love, motivation, and discipline, and you do need those. And you need to exercise that muscle regularly. But all the motivation and discipline in the world will not matter if your limiting beliefs stop you from living your heart's desire. I recently read a quote on X (formerly Twitter) attributed to user Matthew Espinosa: "We cannot shame ourselves into change; we can only love ourselves into evolution." That is exactly what attending masterminds and retreats does for us. To realize sustainable exponential growth, you must look inward and do the really hard work. I am not one to engage in shouting in your face and wearing you down. I believe in releasing your blocks and building you up. My absolute favorite way to expand my mind is with Other People (who would've guessed?). My mastermind group and retreats (my favorite, of course, being the B to the Power of E retreats) are packed with high-level business owners and leaders seeking to develop relationships with their own Other People. Interacting within such a setup will almost certainly lead to brilliant collaborations that propel you towards a well-crafted empire that has the key to growth and success. Once you realize that your circle makes up a large part of your "e," you will see that you need to choose your circle wisely. Be where the people you want to be more like are and be where the people who can help you build your empire are. It is an investment you will make back exponentially.

But it is not just leveraging those Other People's Gifts and Talents; it is also a great way to really explore your own. At one point in my mastermind group, we were asked what we wanted to release and what we wanted more of. One member began to cry because she was worried about giving the wrong answer. Upon further exploration, it was really that she didn't care about the thing she was supposed to care about and really cared about something she seemed to think was somehow less meaningful or important. Be kind and non-judgmental about, and to, yourself. Unless the thing you envision as your dream life, your heart's desire, is harming someone else, there is no wrong answer. Is it just telling people what to do? OK, we do need leaders and visionaries. Is it simple rote tasks because you don't want to have to think too hard while you do them? Those tasks need to be done by someone, so why not you? Is it that you want to create beautiful things? Who doesn't enjoy beautiful things? Do you want to match horses with their ideal people? How truly lovely! Whatever your passion is will be your greatest contribution. And despite the messaging we get growing up and into adulthood, you *can* make a living following your passions if you are strategic, if you plan, if you contribute, and if you find and use OP for the rest. Let me be clear here: You do still need to work hard, and you do need to use your passion to solve people's problems if you want to make money at it. That's the strategy, planning, and contributing part I mentioned.

Investing in Yourself

Growing up, it was ingrained in me to be self-reliant. I don't even know if it was a conscious effort on the part of the well-meaning adults in my life. Probably not. I think they were just doing the best they knew how with the resources they had. When I was around eight or nine, I remember going to my dad and asking for help with my homework. His response was, "You're a smart girl; you can figure it out." That simple statement has stayed with me my whole life. That was literally the only time I ever asked for help with my homework. I *was* a smart girl, and I *did* figure it out. I always got good grades, and that was the goal. Success meant achieving the stated goal on my own and then setting the next one, and so on. And that transcended throughout my life. I thought it was a strength of mine: the grit and tenacity to figure anything out on my own. I was becoming a strong, independent woman, right? Well, sort of. I worked way harder than I needed to just to get to Other People's Ideas of what my goals should be. What? That can't be it. But for most of my life, that was it. I didn't have the confidence to ask for support or feedback. You read that right. It takes confidence in oneself to ask for what you need. You have to know you are enough on your own to be willing to put yourself out there and seek support. And that takes a totally different kind of work that I only recently learned about.

My dad telling me that I was a smart girl and could figure it out was a double-edged sword because I believed him. I have always known I was smart. I have always known I could figure it out. But I have also always believed I had to rely on only that. Until I started investing in myself and allowing myself the support to really grow, that is. Ever hear the term self-made? I think that is a bullshit term. What I have learned on my path toward self-discovery and how to be truly successful is that no one—not me, not you, not your boss, not your partner—no one who is truly successful is completely self-reliant or actually self-made. And I stand by that regardless of what anyone's definition of success is. Because I find it really hard to believe that anyone's definition of success includes being stressed, exhausted, and lonely so long as they achieve whatever it is they seek. How many versions of *A Christmas Carol* does Hallmark need to remake for that lesson to sink in?

When one lives like this, in a bubble of self-reliance, it is more difficult to really soar because the goals are usually smaller. I mean, I had big dreams as a kid, but those were pretty well extinguished by adults who told me to be realistic and responsible. Those same adults demonstrated that success means doing the things that really seemed to me to be just the basics—the starting point, really. And why not? I grew up poor in an area where not many people I knew went to college. Most stayed pretty close to home, and getting married and finding one good job to stay with until retirement was considered success. To be clear, there is nothing wrong with that goal. It just didn't feel like *my* goal. I was told, and for a long time I believed, that the way to achieve success as a smart girl was to go to college and become a doctor or lawyer. So, I went to the only school I thought I could afford and started out pre-med. Nope. It was not for me. In my mind then, there was only one other option: law school.

When it came time to apply for law schools, I looked at it as my ticket out of Ohio. It did not even occur to me that there was another valid, defensible reason to leave. I didn't even apply anywhere in Ohio. When I was accepted to Pepperdine School of Law in California with a scholarship, I accepted before I ever heard back from any other schools. My scarcity mindset was driving me. What if I waited for the others and then Pepperdine somehow changed its collective mind? I better grab my chance while I still had it. I know that does not make any logical sense, and I am largely a logical person, but my soul felt driven by this fear that I would stay put and never realize my full potential.

Upon hearing the news that his daughter had not only been accepted to a good school in beautiful Malibu, California, but had been offered a scholarship, my dad had a fear response of his own: "How the hell are you going to move across the country on your own? How will you afford that? Be realistic." Again reinforcing that idea that I had to figure it out, I decided I was doing it on my own, just like I had done everything to that point, and I would not be talked out of it by anyone, least of all by someone living a life that did not seem to make him very happy. And so I did. I moved to California at the age of 22 with no family or friends, and I started my new life. And I would love to tell you it was all smooth sailing from there, but alas, the big goal was to get to law school, and I had done it. But I hadn't really ever allowed myself to go as big as my soul felt compelled to do. Can you imagine fighting against your heart's desire your whole life because it was impractical and irresponsible? I'll bet most of you can. I think it is more common to squash that little kid's magical thinking than it is to encourage people to be ridiculously optimistic and dream as though nothing is impossible. Why is that? I guess that's for another day and another book.

But I can tell you this: Once you are conscious of this, once you see how you can achieve impossible things if you stop letting fear and old beliefs that aren't even yours anyway drive you, you cannot ignore it. If you really think about it, you will have to realize that nothing great was ever done by playing small, being realistic, or watering down a big, badass vision so it was palatable for people who just can't see what you see. And how fucking cool is it that all of these things or ideas are just ideas? That is to say, they are just thoughts. And what are thoughts but things we make up in our minds? Then I say to you: Decide to make those thoughts big and bold and fun and crazy, and decide for yourself what your thoughts are. Did you know that no one gets to decide your thoughts? I know it seems obvious when I say it like that, but I would venture to say that most of us are largely driven by thoughts handed down to us by our original families, like an old family recipe. Would you keep making that disgusting ambrosia salad your aunt—who smoked over the stove and pinched your cheeks, saying you've put on weight since last year—passed off as a side dish at every holiday gathering once you had your own family and traditions? I doubt it. You can skip the ambrosia salad, and you can skip the limiting beliefs that keep you stuck and small and unhappy. It's just a thought. And thoughts can be changed in your next breath.

What kept driving me was recognizing patterns in myself. For example, each time I pushed myself to achieve a new goal and achieved it, I recognized that it was so much easier than I had imagined it would be. So, the goals got incrementally larger. Not the BHAGs (big, hairy, audacious goals) you have probably been setting for yourself and that I now live by, but bigger than the last at least. So I had two major limitations I placed on myself: 1) I was setting goals that were too small to really get me to the life I knew I wanted, and 2) I was trying to figure out how to achieve those goals all by myself. There were glimpses of my inner goddess trying to get to the surface, but my now-adult brain shut her right up by speaking to her the way I learned that adults speak to dreamy little kids who don't know how the real world works. But she was in there. Waiting. Planning. Dreaming. She would say things like, "I am not sacrificing the things I want forever; I will just make more money." And she would be met with, "Who the hell do you think you are? That is not how responsible adults live. Your salary is what it is, and you work your ass off to maybe get a raise."

And let me tell you, friends, I invested in all the education. I went to college. I went to law school. I consumed self-help books aplenty (even the genre reminded me I was on my own). I learned, and I studied, and I worked hard, and I woke up, and I did it again. Rinse and repeat. Even after reading that famous purple book, Sharon Lechter's and Robert Kiyosaki's *Rich Dad Poor Dad*, it still didn't sink in that working harder than everyone else was not the way to have the kind of life my inner goddess needed. My own deep-seated beliefs were calling the shots. Once I (fill in the next goal here), then I can invest in myself and be free and happy. Here's the thing, though—when you are driven and ambitious and audacious, there is a never-ending supply of next goals.

For many of us, it was Lechter and Kiyosaki who first introduced us to the concept of OPM, or Other People's Money, as a path to true wealth. It is actually one of the concepts that inspired this entire book (maybe not in the way you think). And it's a compelling idea, isn't it? The notion that your fortune can be built using the capital of others. Yet, let me ask you this: What if I were to tell you that the path to your financial empire isn't simply rooted in using OPM? What if the real secret to exponential growth, to conscious wealth creation, and the freedom you desire lies not in doing more but in doing less? Imagine a world where you achieve more by focusing less on the volume of work and more on doing the things you love doing and are amazing at. Would that be interesting to you? That's the power of OPE.

If you are anything like me, you don't mind a little spoiler. So here it is, SPOILER ALERT! To really get to your heart's desire, the goal has to be living your heart's desire, not incremental tasks that get you to some destination where happiness awaits with a pretty bow on it. That destination does not exist. It is a moving target. Whatever your heart's desire is, you have to just BE in it all the time. Easier said than done? Actually, no. Once you say it and believe it, it is already done. You might say, "But, Bethany, if it's so easy, then why doesn't everyone just live their heart's desire?" It's a good question, and I am glad you asked. The answer is conditioning. Mindset. The good news is that it is totally within your control to change. The better news is you get to ask for help in changing it. In fact, you must.

Chapter 2
OPE
Other People's Everything

Remember when I said you have everything you need within you? I know this seems like the antithesis of that, but it's really not. You do. You don't need anything outside yourself to be enough. You are enough. But you do need resources outside yourself to achieve greatness. You need Other People to do that which you don't want to do. What you have is the ability to discern what Other People you need and what you have to offer in turn. Let's explore some of those OPs.

While using Other People's Everything may not be the only way to succeed, it can certainly be an effective strategy for achieving success in many areas. One of the biggest advantages of using Other People's Knowledge, Experience, and Resources is that it saves time. And maybe even more important than time is that by leveraging Other People, you can avoid making the same mistakes they did and streamline your own learning curve. Get to living your magical life faster and more easily? Yes, please. This is not to say you won't make mistakes. You will. But they will be your own fresh mistakes that will save someone else's learning curve when you help them out later. It's the circle of life.

The Power of OPE

When you use Other People's Teams, Networks, and Resources, you can get more done in less time. By tapping into existing structures and systems, you can accomplish your goals faster and more efficiently. I don't know about you, but the idea of working less and making more is appealing to me. My past self would have said that's lazy. She's been fired from making decisions, and she was too tired to fight me on it. The new me is in charge, and she is full of energy because she has OPs galore.

Working with Other People builds relationships and can open up new opportunities for collaboration and growth. By leveraging Other People's Networks, you can expand your own and create new connections that can help you achieve your goals. And the lawyer in me simply cannot get through this without advising you that using Other People's Everything can actually help reduce risk. What? Another benefit of getting help? Yep. By relying on the knowledge and experience of others, you can avoid costly mistakes and minimize the chances of failure.

It took me until way too late in life to decide that building my empire has to be fun, or else why bother? But now that I have made that decision, I have learned that not only is using Other People's Everything more efficient, effective, and easier, it is more fun than doing everything yourself. I used to think competition was the best way to motivate me to get more done, to work harder, and achieve more. Not any longer. Now collaboration is the key. Collaboration allows you to bounce ideas off others, share in the successes, and learn from one another. Celebrating wins with Other People (bragging) is just plain fun. Using Other People's Everything allows you to experience a variety of perspectives, ideas, and approaches. The spice of life and whatnot. This can make your work more interesting and engaging, as you are constantly learning and discovering new things.

Working with Other People can help create a sense of community and belonging. When you work with others, you feel like you are part of something larger than yourself and that you are contributing to a shared vision. I don't think we do this enough. Remote working and prolonged isolation have made it more difficult to achieve a culture of community, which is why we need to make it a conscious priority. When you use Other People's Everything, you have more opportunities to be creative. You can take existing ideas and make them your own or collaborate with others to come up with something entirely new. Checking off tasks is not fun. Creating is fun. Collaborating is fun. And when we are having fun, we don't even notice how damn productive we have been building this empire.

Now, I'm not going to say it's stupid to do everything yourself, mostly because I did that for years and I don't want to be labeled stupid, but it can be inefficient and limiting. No one person can be an expert in everything. By trying to do everything yourself, you may be limiting your potential for success by relying solely on your knowledge and experience. And let's be honest. If you are doing everything, you are doing none of it particularly well.

Achieving Your Goals

In the Entrepreneurial Operating System (EOS), the operating system laid out by Gino Wickman in his book *Traction: Get a Grip on Your Business*, which we use in my law firm, we set rocks. Rocks are 90-day goals that are critical to reaching the longer-term vision. They're called rocks based on the principle that, to maximize space in a jar, you need to add the big rocks first, followed by pebbles, sand, and finally water to fill the gaps. Doing the rocks, or the super important things, first, you ensure they fit. Smaller things fit easily into the crevasses after the big things have been handled. Trying to do every little thing yourself can be incredibly time-consuming, leaving you little time for the truly important tasks. Not everything can be a rock. By leveraging Other People, you can free up time to focus on other aspects of your work or personal life—rocks.

What entrepreneur alive hasn't felt some form of burnout? You know what causes burnout? Doing everything yourself, taking on too much responsibility, and not giving yourself enough time to recharge. By delegating tasks and relying on others, you can avoid burnout and maintain your productivity and well-being.

By not leveraging Other People, you may be missing out on valuable opportunities for growth and success. Working with others can help you expand your network, learn new skills, and access resources and ideas that you may not have been able to on your own. While doing everything yourself is certainly an option, and you may think it's your only option if you are just getting started and think you can't afford help, leveraging Other People can be a more effective and efficient way to achieve your goals and reach your potential for success. You can't afford *not* to use Other People while you pursue your Rocks.

Of course, it's important to note that using Other People's Everything should always be done ethically and legally. It's also important to strike a balance between leveraging Other People's Resources and Ideas and maintaining your own unique identity and vision. Remember, the first step in achieving your extraordinary life and living your heart's desire is to determine what your lane is. That's your unique voice, identity, and vision. Make sure you are putting all these Other People's Ideas and input through your own filter and applying it to your vision. When used appropriately, using Other People's Everything can be a powerful tool for achieving success.

Letting Go of Control

Probably the most important lesson you can learn to scale your business, your wealth, or epic life experiences is to let go of your need to control everything. I know, I know. But don't throw this book away just yet, as I have not completely lost my mind. I see you. I know you feel like if you don't do it, no one will do it as well. After all, you are batshit passionate. Others just won't get it. Am I close?

In *Good to Great*, Jim Collins wrote that good is the enemy of great because of complacency. He and his team of researchers did a deep dive into what was common among companies that made the leap from good to great. They concluded that to become great, there are several key factors we can look to based on this extensive research. One of those critical factors was to remember that people are not your best resource; rather the *right* people are. There are people out there that will work as hard as you work and will be as passionate as you are and whose dreams align with yours, where you can all win. I know, cool, right? And I am here to tell you it's true. He went so far as to say—and the data supports it —that you should choose the people first and *then* assign what they will do. At first, I was a little skeptical too. I was thinking, *Um, Jim, I have this incredible vision that I worked really hard on developing, and now I need the people to help me realize it. You're telling me I did it backward?* I really had to sit with this one for a while before I could accept it.

Here's what I came up with. Yes, I have this vision based on what I want my magical life to be. It took into account my "why" and my ultimate life goals. And my vision took into account what resources I had at the time and what resources I thought I needed to realize it. What it did not contemplate, because how could it ever, was how adding the right people around me could add so much more to my vision than I even imagined. I have chills as I write this. I was actually almost done with the first draft of this book when this hit me for real. I have been building my vision, let's call it Vision 1.0, and this book was part of it. Another part was to build a robust technology platform that could support my law firm clients and create a community where we could leverage each other's expertise and resources, all while really supporting the retreats I want to host. It would streamline the law practice, making it easier for my experienced clients to raise capital and scale their businesses. It would help new entrepreneurs get started building their empires safely.

One of the other concepts in *Good to Great* that really got me was this idea that some leaders or visionaries are the genius with a thousand helpers. That is to say, there are many companies that can grow to be great for a while under the leadership of one brilliant visionary with an army of people to help him/her grow the company, but those companies don't stay great once that leader leaves. To scale and keep it sustainable, the leaders have to empower others to be in their own genius, not just follow the genius of someone else. I want to build a company that continues to be great after I am gone. I want the company to be what is great, and everyone else in the company to thrive.

So, in an effort to be sustainable and scale, my team and I began interviewing technology platforms to Frankenstein together all the things we thought should be included. A piece from this cool company, and some stuff from that one, and so on. Even at the beginning of this process, we were still sorting out who the right people on the bus at the law firm were and making sure they were all in the right seats. There was some housecleaning to do, and it turned out that my biggest supporter in the firm was in the wrong seat. Once we moved her to the operations role, things really began to take off. She started to help me move the right people to the right seats, move the wrong people off the bus (I know cutting people loose can be difficult, but it's necessary—it always has to be the right OPs), and bring in the right people where we had empty seats. Any of you who gets how energy works, doing this automatically opens up space for opportunity to just pour in. And pour it did!

All the meetings we had been having about this technology platform led us to one life-changing realization: The one meeting we thought was going to be a piece of the platform that we had been missing was a meeting with the right Other People... well, person. Jared showed us that his vision and his dream was to build all the things I had dreamed up for this platform, plus a bunch more that I didn't even know was possible! And he had already built most of it. Now, some people might look at this and think, *Oh no, the competition is so much further ahead and already had my idea.* It's OK to admit it; the thought did cross my mind. But this is really important: The right people are never your competition. Read that again: The right people are *never* your competition. The right people are collaborators and co-creators. The right people have aligned visions and values. In this case, these right people had been looking for us as much as we had been looking for them. And so, Vision 1.0 is currently under construction. Because my magical life is not tied to one particular thing, I can be flexible and agile and nimble as to how I get there. I have the freedom to chase these incredible opportunities when they present them-selves because I am paying attention to the Other People around me. I am really seeing their unique gifts and talents and, because I am clear about what mine are, I recognize when someone else fits in where I have gaps. It's not threatening because I was seeking it out.

Even if you have a clear vision, if you don't yet have your dream team, just know there is so much room for that vision to grow beyond your wildest dreams. And, of course, as your busi-ness grows, so too must your team. Continue to surround yourself with a motley crew of talented individuals who not only complement your weaknesses but also share your values and with whom you can have fun.

Out of all the brilliant things you bring to the table, all your talents and gifts and expertise, why is letting go of control the most important thing when scaling your business? For one, your Other People need room to be great. Your team members need the autonomy to make decisions and take ownership of their work. Micromanaging them will not only lead to frustration and stifle their creativity; it's also a complete waste of your efforts and undermines all of your collective brilliance. Why take the time to select all the right Other People and then put them in a cage, so to speak? You don't want to be the genius with a thousand helpers. You want a sustainable business.

Innovation and growth require taking risks and trying new things. If you're too controlling, you are likely also unwilling to take risks, and your business will suffer as a result. Besides, the right Other People will make things you may see as risky safer because they have a different perspective and they know things you don't. You are now free to focus on your strengths and delegate tasks to others who excel in other areas.

That all sounds great, but how the hell do you do it and do it effectively? It'll come as no surprise that the main thing is hiring OPs who are skilled and experienced in their area of expertise, and trusting them to do their job. This will allow you to delegate tasks and free up your time to focus on other aspects of your business. What if your lane is not hiring the right OPs? This one was a real challenge for me in my law firm. I had gotten so busy and became so desperate for help that I hired some of the wrong Other People. This only reinforced my limiting belief that I had to do everything myself because I promptly learned I could not trust these new hires to do their jobs well, so now I was left doing all the work on top of managing mistakes and people who didn't belong in the company at all. And let me be clear, this was all on me. I lacked the right mindset and kept myself stuck just where I already believed I was stuck. And I perpetuated that cycle. And so do you. Yes, you do. We have all done this in one area of our lives or another. So what did I do? I got out of my trusted team members' lanes and let them help me!

Once you have found those OPs, set clear expectations. Communicate clearly with your team about what you expect from them. Inspect what you expect, as author and coach Dan Martell says. This will help ensure that everyone is on the same page and working towards the same goals. If you have not yet determined your vision, you will have to do it if you want to have any hope of scaling. And then you have to let everyone know what it is. Keeping the destination to yourself and the overall culture to be cultivated while heading there will leave everyone toiling aimlessly and, ultimately, lead to stagnation at best, more likely outright failure.

Providing proper training and support to your OPs to help them develop their skills and knowledge is a non-negotiable. Not only will it help them feel more confident and capable, it will make *you* more confident in trusting them to take on more responsibilities. It isn't fair to you or your OPs to leave them without the tools they need to succeed.

It's vital to create systems and processes to help ensure tasks are completed efficiently and effectively. This will reduce the need for micromanaging and allow your team members to work more independently. You cannot scale in any meaningful way until you have this in place. If you don't, you are working way too hard and leaving too much room for error. Admittedly, this can be a big up-front lift, but once it is complete, you will wonder how you ever survived without it. Before we had expanded our team and brought on the help we needed at the law firm, everything we did was in either my partner's or my head. That means that everything that needed to be done had to at least start off on one of our plates.

Hard to scale when nothing can get done without you involved. It actually became a point of pride for us when there was something within the firm we didn't even know how to do (not legal-related, don't worry).

Scaling your business requires letting go of control. This can be a difficult lesson to learn, but it's crucial for success. By hiring the right people, setting clear expectations, providing training and support, and creating systems and processes, you can safely let go of control while still ensuring your business is running smoothly. Please note, as you scale, your role will shift from doing everything yourself to leading and guiding your team towards success. Embrace this shift and trust your team to help you achieve your goals.

Delegate, Delegate, Delegate

You're not Iron Man, despite your brilliant ingenuity. OK, maybe you sort of are, but even Iron Man had Dr. Ho Yinsen. And Pepper. And the Avengers. You get the idea. As the mastermind behind your growing empire, you must learn to let go of certain tasks and responsibilities. Yes, that means trusting your (maybe newly minted) dream team to handle matters without your constant supervision. Remember, even the most powerful superheroes can't take on all the bad guys alone. So, give your team a chance to shine while you focus on what you can best control.

Scaling a business is no easy feat. As you grow, you'll need to learn new skills or hone some old ones, make tough decisions, and manage some of those Other People. But as we have already established, the most important lesson you can learn to scale your business is to let go of control. Letting go of control means you have to delegate every single task that is not in pure alignment with your unique superpowers. All of them. Yes, even that one thing that you do well, but actually hate doing.

Once you know exactly who you are and what you do want to do, and once you have all the right Other People in all the right seats, delegating is easy. It's easy because all you have to do is stop doing what is not yours to do. Stop jumping into Other People's lanes. The right people already want to do it. When you are so in your zone and everyone else is in theirs, it is almost impossible not to kick ass. Everyone is happy and contributes to their highest capacity.

Chapter 3
OPJ
Other People's Junk

Before we dive into all the Other People's stuff you can leverage to build your empire, we should address the nasty qualities of Other People that you should not adopt as your own. Do you remember earlier when I mentioned negative exponential function? In this context, that happens when we take on Other People's shit that diminishes our "B," our constant. The more negative or harmful input you feed into the "B," the more exponential damage you can do. That is not the way we are headed to build your empire.

As an entrepreneur, you may, *and should,* be constantly looking for ways to leverage Other People's Resources to grow your business. But before you start taking everything that comes your way, it's important to consider what Other People's stuff you *don't* want. Be discerning. Be mindful. Be downright picky. What are some examples of what we don't want?

I mean, there's the super obvious stuff, like you don't need to take Other People's old, broken garbage. Sure, your friend may be offering you their old computer for free, but is it really worth it? Outdated technology can slow down your business and cause unnecessary headaches. Don't be shortsighted here. I was half joking, but Other People's old, broken garbage can take many forms.

Whose goals are you working so hard to achieve? If you haven't taken the hard step of determining exactly what *you* want, you are working for someone else, whether you think you are or not.

Other People's Responsibilities

Taking responsibility for your SELF, while it can be difficult at first, is freeing, even if that responsibility is for choosing the wrong Other People. Own your shit. The flip side of this, though, is that while you are busy staying in your own lane, attending to your own unique gifts and talents, and maintaining your power, you will not be taking on what Other People ought to be doing, and you will not be borrowing responsibility that does not belong to you. It may seem easier to just do it yourself. And you may feel some sense of obligation to the Other People you bring into the fold to help them. As a number two on the Enneagram, The Helper, this has been a lifelong challenge of mine. This is why it is so critical to dig deep and learn exactly what you should be doing and trust yourself and your Other People. Even if you see people flailing in all the other lanes, if it is not your lane, it does not help them if you jump in it. All that is going to do is drag you all under. I am not saying don't help people. I am saying do it from your own lane by doing what you do best, not by trying to do what they should have been doing.

"When you take responsibility for your thoughts, feelings, and behaviors, you get your power back. Your life is yours to live. Your power is yours to keep. You don't have to give it away to anyone."
–Healing Energy Tools, online musical artist

The Power of OPE

Several years ago, I left the practice of law to join a woman I knew and trusted to help launch a fund with a genius, albeit complicated, structure that I helped develop as the attorney. I did all the right things: She had already assembled a team of people to do most of the things that a fund required, so I was walking into an existing infrastructure. I made sure to cover my bases so there was no conflict of interest; since I had been practicing law and former clients were involved, I had the relevant people seek counsel of their own, and I did all the legal research on the fund model and structure I had designed to make sure it worked for its intended purpose. On paper, this was brilliant. I would achieve my dream of having a fund that developed real estate in areas needing jobs while bringing those jobs into the area through a technology accelerator. Even better, those start-ups we invested in and accelerated would have female and underrepresented founders and leadership teams. My heart was in the right place, my brain did the heavy lifting, and we were off! Except that we weren't. Some investors did not understand the complicated model, even when we plainly laid it out. Or, and this is probably more important, most real estate investors don't live in the same body as tech start-up investors, and this fund was both. Oh, and it was right before the 2016 election, so just a weird time all around. Plenty went wrong.

Fast forward to a fund I organized that failed to get off the ground and resulted in some very angry partners who had put up significant money to get this thing launched. I was devastated. I had failed. No, I was a failure. My gremlin was taking over (see *The Wise Investor: A Modern Parable About Creating Financial Freedom and Living Your Best Life* by Rich Fettke for more on this). Even after the initial capital was gone, I continued working tirelessly to try to make this fund work. I pivoted, restructured, and tried everything I could think of so my partners would not be out their money. And I did this for no pay. My savings was gone, my credit was shot, my confidence was destroyed, and my mindset vacillated between victim and martyr.

While it wasn't my fault the fund failed, it was at least partially my responsibility to deal with the aftermath. What wasn't my responsibility, which I didn't consider at the time, was to keep myself stuck in this sinking ship, no-win situation, not allowing myself the opportunity to succeed in the future because I had failed in the past. It was not my responsibility to single-handedly make back my partners' money at the expense of my own well-being and livelihood. They were angry, sure, and I understand that. But with some time and distance between then and now, I have learned so much about that situation. They were trying to place blame for many things going on in their lives, and the fund had little to do with it. My real failure wasn't that the fund lost money; we were all in that together. My real failure was not being more selective when choosing my Other People in the first place (and maybe they could say the same of me). I should have been much quicker to replace my Other People when it became evident things were not working. Author and speaker Wayne Dyer was right on the money when he said, "You can't feel bad enough to make anybody else's life better." My guilt and fear over a situation completely out of my control created some really hard times and set me back years on my goals. But the lessons I learned were invaluable. One such lesson is that it does no one any good when you take responsibility that does not belong to you.

Other People's Opinions

Many have said that what Other People think of you is none of your business. Good or bad, being influenced by Other People's Opinions can derail your growth and leave you without a healthy sense of self. If who you are is wrapped up in trying to stop people from thinking poorly of you or trying to make people think highly of you, you become a performer in your own life. Your every move becomes calculated to influence someone else rather than to propel you closer to your heart's desire. Likewise, if you are waiting for Other People to tell you what to think about any given topic, you are giving away your power to be your authentic self. And, I hate to break it to you, but this is a game you can never win. You will never be everyone's favorite, and you will never be able to choose all the "correct" opinions from Other People to be your best self. Why? Because you are the best at being you. You would suck at being me, and my opinions on anything are really only good for me being me. Likewise, I cannot adopt your opinions as my own.

Don't get me wrong; I think we all need to learn from Other People. I am writing an entire book on the concept. But we can hear people's thoughts, run them through our filters, and then use that data to formulate our educated opinions. Modern news-makers count on the fact that we will simply ingest opinions cast at us if said loudly enough or with enough conviction. This is a dangerous game, and I urge you not to play it. When you really get to know yourself, learning your unique gifts and talents and what you truly love, that process will help you realize you have every-thing you need to take in all the information, including opinions of others, and distill it down to something that is meaningful to you. And what is meaningful to you, when delivered in your most authentic way, is meaningful to others as well.

In this age of social media, with total strangers blasting their opinions at you every time you look at your phone, it can be hard to hear your own opinions over all the noise. You wouldn't trust a total stranger to take your children for the week or even drive your car, so why would you make important life decisions based solely on the opinion of someone else? Being influenced by Other People's Opinions can limit your ability to make decisions based on your own judgment and reasoning, which often leads to a lack of confidence and self-reliance. And this can become even more problematic when those opinions are from people you know and love.

I struggled with my self-confidence as a young woman. I sought validation from others as a way to justify my very existence. This took many forms. Sometimes it was trying to look a certain way, other times it was to prove I was the smartest, and other times it was to show I was the hardest worker. No matter what I did, there was no amount of praise or attention I could get that would make me feel worthy of whatever it was I wanted in that moment. Not from anyone else. Not my parents, or love interests, or teachers, or bosses.

When I was young, an adult in my life I looked up to told me I was too smart to be creative. I think he meant well. I want to believe he was trying to steer me toward a career path he thought would make my life easier somehow. As I mentioned, we were poor, and many people in my life thought toiling was the only way to get out of poverty, despite all the evidence that even that didn't work, or else all the hardworking people I knew would never worry about money. So, I grew up thinking being creative and being smart were mutually exclusive. Can you imagine? Leonardo Da Vinci, in addition to being a painter and a sculptor, was an engineer, scientist, theorist, and architect. I didn't know this at the time, or my smartass self might have had a better response than quiet resignation that I shouldn't pursue music, or comedy, or writing. What if someone Da Vinci loved and respected told him painting was frivolous and he should just focus on engineering? Even worse, what if he *believed* them? There would be no Mona Lisa. No Last Supper. I'm not saying I would have been Da Vinci, but I'm also not saying I couldn't have been. What I am saying is that if we get so wrapped up in Other People's Opinions, particularly opinions of what you should or should not dream about and pursue as your heart's desire, you may deprive the world of your ideas, possibilities, and gifts. You may limit your growth and development while you are focused on pleasing others instead of working on your personal and professional goals. You may find it difficult for others to connect with you when you are constantly seeking validation and approval because it is hard to know the real you when you are simply reflecting Other People back at them.

Other People's Baggage

What do I mean by baggage? This is anything that anyone you know has brought with them from any past trauma or difficulty that keeps them from living in their heart's desire. It can be limiting beliefs from their childhood, bad habits or behaviors picked up along the way, toxic relationships that follow them, or anything they hold on to that does not serve them in the best possible way. Other People's Baggage can cause a severe emotional drain on you. Everyone has a past. Some people are better at coping with theirs than others, and some people have had a more difficult past than others.

Take a moment to think about anything from your past that you've brought with you into the future. Do you need it all? Does it limit your ability to grow or find true happiness? What are you doing to reduce your own baggage? Now think about every person you know. We all have baggage we have not yet consolidated to a reasonable carry-on size. But each person's baggage is their responsibility to carry, check, or leave behind. They do not get to just hand it to you to carry for them. They should use Other People to help, sure, and you may be one of those people. But please report any unattended items and do *not* pick them up. If they refuse to unpack it, assume it is a bomb and leave it. And while we are using cheesy air travel metaphors, let's not forget the one about putting on your own mask before helping others. If you are so focused on Other People's Baggage, you will inevitably lose track of your own goals and dreams while you are sorting out how to diffuse a bomb you didn't bring to the party.

A friend of mine dated a woman who was divorced with three children. Not super uncommon. But the red flag popped up when this woman routinely badmouthed her ex-husband to him and blamed him for everything that went wrong in her life. They had been divorced for years, yet he was a constant topic, and it was never positive. She spent excessive energy hating him, fighting with him, and complaining to my friend about him. My friend, trying to be a good partner, jumped right into it with her. Defending her position and complaining with her, it was like he'd been married to this guy. It got to a point where my friend, who only knew this guy through his girlfriend, would get into verbal altercations with him. It took up his energy, it tainted his relationship with his girlfriend, and I heard all about it even though it was absolutely none of my business. If I were a betting woman, I would wager that I was not the only friend who got an earful about this relationship. Finally, I had to call him out. If I wanted to watch a reality show, I would choose one with much more interesting characters, but I am busy building an empire and do not have time for this nonsense.

You can probably guess how much work my friend did on himself or how much he focused on his passions while he was in this relationship. If I'm being honest, he really didn't have a free hand to carry anyone else's baggage because his was still a bit heavy. But dealing with hers distracted him from his. This may have been a short-term relief from his own shit, but being weighed down by Other People's Baggage limited his ability to cope with his own issues and setbacks.

What was worse was that while my friend was so focused on his girlfriend's baggage, his other relationships suffered. It caused a strain with his own kids; his friends distanced themselves, and his family worried for him. While he meant well and thought he was being supportive and helping, he was just enabling her to continue on with a toxic situation. She dragged them both down. Had my friend simply refused to take on her baggage and either insisted she deal with it herself or opted out of the relationship altogether, which was the end result anyway, he could have saved both of them so much heartache and all the Other People in his life that were negatively impacted.

It's important to be aware of the impact of Other People's Baggage on your own well-being and to take steps to manage it. Set boundaries, seek support, and practice self-care. Use your healthy Other People to help. The common theme here is to allow yourself to really know and see yourself and honor yourself first. You get to be a little selfish here. This world is better for having a healthy and happy you in it.

Choose Other People carefully, and which of their *things* you want to leverage. You are not a bellhop. You do not need to carry Other People's Baggage. In fact, you should not even be carrying your own baggage. The trip to conscious wealth requires you to travel light.

Other People's Drama

This one is very similar to Other People's Baggage. I have noticed throughout my life that there are people who would rather be distracted by someone else's drama than focus on their own growth and personal and professional development. As with everything else we have been talking about, if you are clear about who you are and what lights you up, you will no longer have room for Other People's Drama because you will be too busy focusing on your own goals and priorities. But if you would rather stay in someone else's shit, it'll only slow you down and frustrate you. A solid empire cannot be built upon such a shoddy foundation.

Everyone says they hate drama, but you really need to take

active steps to ban it from your life. It's a distraction. Nothing more. We all have that friend where it's always something with them. And if you don't have that friend, there's a good chance you are that friend. Every time you talk to them, they have a new crisis: their boyfriend is a jerk, the boss sucks, someone rear-ended their car, their purse got stolen again, Mercury is in retrograde, or whatever. Sometimes it's hard to stay out of it because it seems legitimate, and they're genuinely upset, and you don't want to be a bad friend or family member. But if you watch the patterns, you will see that some people just invite drama in. Or, whenever bad stuff happens, because bad stuff happens to every one of us, it can't just be a bad thing that happened, and they cope, learn, and move on. Not with this friend. With this friend, it is all a catastrophic calamity that requires hours of pontification and a rallying of everyone they know and maybe a film crew. They will spend hours on the phone with you, hashing through every detail. They may not even ask you for advice. They just talk. And you just listen. And listen. And listen some more.

I used to have a friend where we would be talking, and sometimes I would think, *Oh, I've heard this one before,* and I would start doing something else and just occasionally toss in a "That's crazy" or "No way!" She never even noticed. But as I was working through some of my own struggles in my one-on-one meetings with Susan, and I brought this up as a frustration, she asked, "What is the win in it?"

I replied, "Excuse me? I just said I was frustrated by it and that it eats up time and energy that I simply cannot afford to waste. What do you mean, what's the win in it?"

Susan said (and she said this about a lot of my issues I got stuck on, so this may be applicable to several chapters): "There must be some win in it for you, or else you would have let it go by now." Well, fuck. So even this one was on me? But remember what

I said earlier: The good news about my garbage is I get to control it and correct it.

"So what do I do? I am a helper. I am a good friend. I am loyal. I can't just abandon that and be selfish. My friend needs me." As I said this to her, she just smiled at me. I won't say it was a condescending smile exactly, but in these moments, a knowing smile can feel a little like an attack when I don't want to be called out. We have been working together long enough that she knows I will eventually get there myself with her prompting. My win was that I thought it was my value to be a helper. To be a good friend. To be loyal. It is. But it is not my value to be those things at my own expense. And I wasn't even really being any of those things. Hours of conversation went by, and I didn't hear half of it. I didn't have the bandwidth for it. I was being dishonest with my friend and actually kind of mean to myself by not just setting a boundary, and saying I didn't have capacity for this right now. I was half-ass focused on her drama and half-ass focused on whatever else I was doing, and neither of them got the best of me. I was frustrated, and my friend was no better off as a result.

My sister, Danielle, and I have a deal. When either of us needs to vent or needs support, we ask permission first. "Do you have the capacity for me to vent right now?" And we give each other permission to say no, and that's okay. Anyone in your life who truly loves and respects you will also respect your boundaries. I am not suggesting you have to cut everyone who has a proclivity for drama out of your life. But once you have taken the time and energy to truly know yourself and what your goals are and what your heart's desire is, you will find it necessary, maybe even easy, to set clear and healthy boundaries to insulate yourself from Other People's Drama. Those people may self-select out once you have set those ground rules, or you may decide you have to limit your connection to them, but once you do that, you are honoring yourself and agreeing not to feed your constant, your base, a negative exponential function in the form of drama.

Other People's Negativity

This is a big one. A negative mindset can create devastating consequences if left unchecked. In Kurt Vonnegut's satirical postmodern novel *Cat's Cradle*, the fictional substance Ice 9 was created at the behest of the government to solve a mud problem. The intentions were arguably good, but the result was apocalyptic. Ice 9 could cause water to turn to ice at room temperature just by its contact. What could go wrong, right? Eventually there was an accident, and Ice 9 was dropped into the ocean, freezing all the water on Earth and everything that water touched or had water in it. Even people who didn't immediately die ultimately killed themselves, believing it was inevitable.

I know it may seem alarmist and perhaps a bit far-reaching, but I think we can draw some similarities between negativity and Ice 9. Mere contact with either can turn that which is otherwise stable, even life-giving, into something dangerous. There are the obvious consequences of a negative impact on mental health and well-being, like stress, anxiety, and depression. And then there are the more subtle ramifications, such as an inability to recognize a different perspective, limiting your ability to see things from a healthier point of view, and resulting in a narrow and rigid mindset that isn't well equipped to deal with life as it presents you with obstacles. If you adopt Other People's Negativity, your creativity and ability to think outside the box may be diminished.

When the Ice 9 had frozen all the water, leaving the remaining people unable to see any positive outcome, they lost their drive and initiative to carry on. Likewise, adopting Other People's Negativity can limit your motivation, which will kill that drive and initiative that keeps you pushing toward your dream life each day.

I am a firm believer that a positive mindset is stronger than a negative one, but a positive mindset actually requires attention and practice, whereas a negative mindset, unfortunately, can creep in when you aren't looking. If you knew someone had the potential to create such havoc as Ice 9, causing you to flail when faced with challenges and setbacks rather than to rise up and adapt, hurting your relationships and your ultimate success, how would you treat that person? Would you let them drag you under, or would you contain them, not allowing them to infect your mindset? I know a lot of you want to answer that you will pull them up, and I commend you for that. But I caution you: A negative person has to want to be pulled up, and mere contact with negativity can spread like Ice 9, so please proceed with caution.

Our brains are wired for survival—to fight or flee, not for happiness and fulfillment. We have to teach them to be happy and to thrive. Practicing mindfulness, setting boundaries, and surrounding yourself with positive influences are such simple and effective tools for this. Positive affirmations are a good start, but deep work on your own limiting beliefs will give you the best chance at success.

"If you don't know where you are going, any road will take you there."
–Lewis Carroll

Other People's Goals

Anyone reading this book already knows that setting goals is critical to success. We need to affirmatively decide where we are headed to know if we got there. For a goal to be meaningful to you and therefore attainable by you, it has to be your own, driven by whatever your heart's desire is. That's why it is so critical that you know what your heart's desire is. If you don't, you run the risk of setting goals that are really Other People's misplaced expectations

43

of you, which are not designed to get you to where you want to be going; rather, they are designed to satisfy a perceived obligation. Other People's goals may not align with your own values, interests, and priorities, which means that unless you also have that other person's motivation and commitment to achieving them, you will probably be wandering aimlessly with the delusion that you have a clear path and purpose. Pursue what lights you up.

Setting goals is not a check-the-box situation. Simply writing down things one might achieve with no greater purpose or meaning behind them is nothing more than an exercise and will not get you to your ultimate vision for your magical life. You may have noticed a theme brewing here, which is that the first step to building your empire and creating your magical life is getting really honest with yourself about what that looks like. Not what your parents expect it to look like. Not what your friends think it should be like. Maybe not even what you thought it was going to look like when you first started on this adventure. Dream. Imagine. Suspend judgment. Then commit. Unapologetically and authentically, scream your heart's desire from the proverbial rooftops. Because if you don't, you will be working toward someone else's vision. And what fun is that?

When I got to law school, that was really as far as I had dared vision. My goal was to get there, and I had. Or, to put it more honestly, my goal was to leave Ohio, and I did. Not being in a place is not as fulfilling as achieving a long-term goal. Graduating was an obvious goal, so I didn't even bother thinking about that. But then what? I had never allowed myself to dream big before, and moving to California and going to Pepperdine seemed like the biggest thing I was allowed to dream. I didn't particularly love the idea of being a lawyer—it was just better than being poor, and I didn't think I would make a good doctor. During law school, it seemed the obvious goal of most students was to get hired at a big law firm. For a few, it was to be a law professor, but that sounded absolutely dreadful to me. So, I adopted most Other People's goal of being hired in a big law firm. I didn't know how I was going to do that, but it was a goal.

Now, to get courted by big law firms, you really needed to come from a top school. Pepperdine was a decent school, but it wasn't Ivy League, so students really had to stand out to be offered summer associate positions. Those really sounded fun, because they took you to fancy lunches and let you work on sexy cases and lured you into this false sense of glamor of being a first-year associate. Because this wasn't really *my* goal but rather a goal I had adopted as my own, I wasn't particularly motivated to achieve it. I didn't own it. Early on, I recall one of our professors telling us that the A students would become professors, the B students would become partners in a big law firm, and the C students would make all the money. We all laughed, but I think it was lost on most of us. I mean, part of me was like, *Sweet, why kill myself to be an A or even a B student when I really wanted to make a lot of money?* I kept it to myself because it was crass to say you were money motivated, and it might give away that I'd never had money. None of my peers admitted they wanted anything other than the professorship or partner track. To get anything less would be deemed a failure.

I was a C student in law school, which was not surprising given I was only going through the motions. I was not courted for a summer associate position, and I did not apply to any. My then boyfriend showed me a listing for an in-house clerkship making $15 an hour. I was afraid I wasn't even qualified for that, but he encouraged me to apply anyway. I got the job! It wasn't sexy or glamorous, but I actually liked it. I met some great mentors, and I ended up meeting my now ex-husband there. That's a happier story than it seems; it led to my daughter, who is my world.

I was off track with this goal of going to Big Law, but I still had this nagging feeling inside me that it was what I was supposed to want. Still, I never really followed through on making it happen the traditional way. As it turned out, the place where I was clerking used a big firm as outside counsel. We were one of their biggest clients. My mentor asked them to interview me, and while they never hired true associates this way (they had a pedigree to protect), they did have contract attorneys that worked there on an hourly basis. It wouldn't be the huge money that first-year associates made, and I missed out on some of the sexy perks of being wooed, but I made it into a big law firm on a technicality, and it was still way more money than I had ever made by far. Why wasn't I happier? I told myself it was because I hadn't truly achieved the goal, and I wasn't good enough to even get the job I really wanted. So, I worked myself to death to prove I belonged at a job I didn't truly love and that didn't light me up.

The truth was, had I really gotten honest about what I wanted, I would have had to admit this wasn't it. It was around this time that I dove back into the kind of personal development and entrepreneurial books that I had enjoyed back in college, and I had this itch to explore something else. But while I was there, I toiled away and didn't explore other passions or develop the skills I would later need to become a real estate investor and entrepreneur. I didn't enjoy that sense of accomplishment and satisfaction that I later learned was like a drug when you are pursuing something meant just for you and your dreams.

I wasn't my best self; I was not unapologetically and authentically me. And my confidence was still shaky from feeling like I got this job by mistake and was a fraud within the firm. I was not being true to myself and therefore felt like I lacked integrity.

I learned plenty while I was at that firm, sure. And because I am happy with my life now, I can't say I regret it. But I will admit that I believe that the job distracted me from setting my own goals and delayed me dreaming up my heart's desire. Partly because all I did was work, but also because I didn't yet have the appropriate mindset to dare to dream so big. So, here I was, having achieved what was supposed to be the big goal, and I was burned out, feeling unsatisfied and insecure. Because this was really Other People's goal I had achieved, I was not fully invested in it and definitely did not have the same level of commitment as someone who really had this as her goal.

So, I left. I went out on my own and set up my own firm. I swung *all* the way out. That was also the result of not having done the work to decide my vision, but I eventually learned. Stick with me. I will help you shortcut what took me years to power through.

Chapter 4
OPM
Other People's Money

The idea of using OPM is not new. The article titled "The Surest Path to Success is Other People's Money," first published in *The Sunday Times* on January 31, 2016, rightfully pointed out: "MOST of those who become very rich share a particular secret about the accumulation of wealth: they use OPM... It is a far more important tool than brilliant inventiveness, hard work, or almost any of the other attributes that entrepreneurs are expected to possess." And while I agree with this notion, I think I have demonstrated that it is not enough on its own. Still, it is necessary, so let's talk about it.

I first learned about the concept of OPM during all the reading I was doing while I was figuring out what the hell I was doing at that big law firm (although the concept would not sink in for quite some time). It is a concept that all of my real estate investor clients live by. I have made a good bit of my money from Other People using OPM. It's like a dream within a dream. Or something. Anyway, in 1914, U.S. Supreme Court Justice Louis Brandeis wrote the book *Other People's Money and How the Bankers Use It*. While it wasn't a glowing review of *how* bankers used OPM, he pointed out that OPM is even better than having a goose that lays golden eggs because it amounts to "taking the golden eggs laid by somebody else's goose."

As far back as 1776, the economist Adam Smith warned in his book *The Wealth of Nations* that human nature may mean that when managing OPM, people would never steward it with the "anxious vigilance" they would with their own. However, he went on to recommend to young entrepreneurs that they cultivate their ability to leverage OPM because it is the "surest path to financial success."

Whoever gets credit for encouraging entrepreneurs to use OPM to build their empires was right. But one must also heed their warnings. Human nature being what it is, and the U.S. government being what it is, whole bodies of law sprung up to protect those Other People from those of us wanting to use their money. And that's where I come in: a securities lawyer helping entrepreneurs practice safe SEC. Sounds fun, right? Actually, I love it. It allows me to take my place as the trusted advisor, the mage, if you will, to the people creating, building, doing, cultivating, and conjuring. It allows me to do all those things as well.

If using OPM is so scary and can lead to bad behavior and has led to all these laws, you may be wondering why the heck you would even want to use it in the first place. I'll tell you why: Creating wealth should not just be for the already ultra-wealthy, and their secret is that they leverage OPM! Even multi-millionaires. Even billionaires. Even if they were born with it. All of them. And if they can use it to create even *more* wealth, then you can use it to create yours from scratch. So long as you do so conscientiously and within the guardrails your Other People set up for you. Remember, all you need is education, mindset, and access to opportunities. And don't let your limiting mindset stop you from accessing opportunities that you thought were out of reach, reserved for only the elite, or because you are afraid. Your OPs have got you!

Now is the part you have to bear with me. I am, after all, a lawyer, so some parts of this get a little dense. I trust you'll hang in there because this is really juicy information you need. If you are already a pro at leveraging OPM, feel free to skip ahead. But, hey, a little refresher is always good, so I hope you press on. OK, so let's break this down into a few of its basic components.

The Different Forms of OPM

While my lane as it relates to OPM is primarily private securities offerings, I will touch on the various ways you can leverage OPM to scale your business. Keep in mind, the U.S. Securities and Exchange Commission (SEC) could even get involved if your OPM is not structured properly, so part of my lane is to keep you out of that world if that is your intent. I help you practice safe SEC if you are ready to engage in SEC, but you should only do so with someone you trust and when you are really ready. And if you are not ready, I can help you effectively abstain from SEC.

One common way to leverage OPM is to borrow it from a lender, such as a bank or other financial institution. This can be done through a loan or a line of credit, and the borrowed funds can be used to purchase properties, make investments, or fund other business activities. These "traditional" bank loans, or debt financing, have long been a popular source of OPM for entrepreneurs. These loans involve borrowing a specific amount of money from a bank and repaying it over time with interest. Bank loans can provide the necessary capital for startups, expansions, or major investments. However, they often require collateral, a strong credit history, and a well-defined business plan to secure approval. And I'm not sure if you've been paying attention, but the interest rates available to you can fluctuate widely, even after you have received the loan, so this option is better at some times than others. Still, if you plan appropriately and surround yourself with OPs that have navigated this world before, you can really make the most of traditional finance.

Do not listen to those old-school financial "experts" who tell you debt is bad! Good debt is a tool of the rich. Good debt is debt that is used to acquire an asset that makes you more than the debt costs you. It's simple math. Math not your lane? OPE. Debt to buy things that do not make you money, like flashy cars and toys, is bad debt and can be disastrous if you don't have passive income to pay for it. And this is definitely an area where already being wealthy is yet another chip stacked in one's favor, since lenders tend to give better terms to those who don't need to borrow. But I am no longer angry about that fact. I am educated, and I have shifted my mindset, and I know there are creative tools available to me. One such tool, er, OP, which I will discuss in more detail under Other People's Credit later in this chapter, is a key principal (KP) and can be an invaluable resource to you if you are just getting started in borrowing OPM.

Private money lending, also known as peer-to-peer lending or private lending, is a way of leveraging OPM by borrowing from private individuals or groups instead of traditional financial institutions. One significant advantage private money lending offers is that private lenders often have more flexible lending criteria compared to traditional financial institutions, making it easier for entrepreneurs with limited credit history or unconventional business models to secure funding. Private money lending also provides a faster and more streamlined application process, allowing entrepreneurs to access capital quickly. However, there are potential drawbacks to consider. Regulatory risks are a significant concern in private lending, as the industry is subject to evolving regulations that may affect loan terms, interest rates, and investor protections. Entrepreneurs must carefully navigate these regulatory landscapes to ensure compliance and mitigate potential legal risks. Additionally, private money lending often comes with higher interest rates compared to traditional bank loans, which can increase the overall cost of borrowing. Therefore, you should carefully assess the risks and benefits before engaging in private money lending.

Hard money lending, a form of private lending that focuses on providing short-term loans secured by real estate, has its own set of pros and cons for entrepreneurs seeking OPM. One major advantage is the speed at which funds can be obtained. Like private money, hard money lenders typically have a streamlined application and approval process, allowing entrepreneurs to access capital quickly, which can be particularly beneficial for time-sensitive real estate projects. Hard money lenders are also more flexible in their lending criteria, considering factors such as the property's value and potential profitability rather than strict creditworthiness. However, there are certain disadvantages to consider. Hard money loans also often come with higher interest rates and fees compared to traditional bank loans or even other private money loans, increasing the overall cost of borrowing. Additionally, regulatory risks can pose challenges in hard money lending, as laws and regulations surrounding real estate financing vary by jurisdiction. As always, you need to have OPs around you to guide you through the regulatory landscape to ensure compliance and mitigate potential legal risks when engaging in hard money lending. It is crucial to weigh these factors and evaluate the specific needs and circumstances of the business before opting for hard money loans as a source of OPM.

Various forms of selling a piece of your business—commonly referred to as equity—are different from debt. One of these is angel investors. Angel investors are individuals who invest their personal capital into early-stage businesses in exchange for equity or ownership stakes. They typically provide mentorship, industry expertise, and networking opportunities, along with financial support. Angel investors are often drawn to high-potential startups and can be an excellent source of OPM, especially when the business is still in its infancy. These are some really valuable OPs if your company has a really high upside potential. Most of my current clients are in real estate, and angel investors typically flock to traditional startups in tech, consumer products, or other operating companies. Still, if you have access to an angel, they can be a great resource.

Venture capitalists (VCs) are firms or individuals who invest large sums of money in businesses with high growth potential. Unlike angel investors, VCs typically manage pooled funds from various other investors. They often invest in exchange for equity and expect a significant return on their investment. VCs are more likely to invest in established businesses with proven traction and a scalable business model. Like angel investors, VCs tend to gravitate toward traditional operating companies over real estate since the potential returns are much higher (as is the risk in most cases). In my opinion, the VC model is flawed and favors the already wealthy, but it remains a potential source of OPM for a select few. If you have a rosy anecdotal experience to share about VCs, please be sure to let me know by sending me a DM on Instagram at @bethany_laflam or dropping a comment in the Collective Lounge at Conscious Capital Collective (https://consciouscapital collective.mn.co/).

An often-overlooked source of OPM are the various governments and organizations that provide grants and funding programs to support entrepreneurial initiatives. These grants are often awarded based on specific criteria, such as industry focus, innovation, or social impact. Government funding can be an excellent source of OPM, as it doesn't require repayment and can provide a significant boost to a business's growth prospects. It takes some effort and research to find and apply for government funding, but it's so worth the effort if it aligns with your business goals. You may even hire a virtual assistant to help you source these grants and prepare applications. All the OPs, baby!

This next one can be tricky if you aren't careful. Take it from a securities lawyer that you have to structure these properly to steer clear of securities law violations. But with proper guidance, strategic partnerships and joint ventures (JVs) can allow entrepreneurs to tap into OPM by collaborating with other businesses or individuals in a powerful way. This approach involves sharing resources, expertise, and even customer bases to achieve mutually beneficial goals. By leveraging the strengths of each partner (hello, OPE!), entrepreneurs can access additional capital, distribution channels, or technological advancements without taking on additional debt or diluting ownership beyond the partners. JVs can be a way of leveraging OPM by partnering with other investors or business operators alongside you. In this case, each partner provides the capital, and the venture is typically structured as a partnership or limited liability company.

Be careful not to take passive investors' money and call it a JV. If the money source is relying on your efforts to provide a return, you have likely sold securities and must comply with securities laws. Yes, even your rich uncle giving you the money can be a securities offering. Seek guidance from a qualified attorney when structuring any kind of business arrangement, and make sure you choose one who is knowledgeable in the area you need. Something to remember here is that being a JV and being a securities offering are mutually exclusive. More on this later in the chapter.

For startups or early-stage operating companies, incubators and accelerators are organizations that provide support and resources while they are just getting going. They often offer workspace, mentorship, training, and access to investors. By joining an incubator or accelerator program, entrepreneurs can gain valuable connections and secure funding from the organization or its network of investors, effectively leveraging OPM. There will probably be more funding required once you get going, but this can be a good launchpad to get your business going if the upside potential is really high.

And finally, we get to one of my personal favorite ways to leverage OPM: raising capital through the sale of equity in your business, such as stocks or partnership interests, to private individuals (as opposed to angel investors and VCs discussed above). This can be done through an initial public offering (IPO), which is somewhat rare, expensive, and time-consuming, or a private placement (much more relevant to most of you reading this), and the funds raised can be used to purchase properties, make investments, or fund other business activities. While raising capital can be an exciting milestone, it comes with risks and responsibilities. You will enter the realm of securities offerings, which involves legal obligations. Investors trust you with their hard-earned money, expecting a return on their investment, so it's essential to be transparent when communicating the potential risks associated with your deal. This is a formal requirement and process, so consult with legal and tax professionals well-versed in securities law to ensure compliance.

Selling securities is not like selling anything else—you have to learn the rules of this new game. Two big examples of this are paying people to raise capital and advertising—it's harder than most people think, but not impossible with the right team. Since this is largely my lane, I will dive a little deeper here. First of all, let's talk about what selling securities even is. Importantly, the way the SEC determines whether an instrument is a security often relies on the economic reality of the transaction rather than the name of the instrument. Meaning, you don't get to call the transaction something else (say, a promissory note or a JV) just to avoid having to comply with securities laws. This determination is typically made using the Howey Test, which originates from a

Supreme Court case and says that a transaction is an investment contract (and thus a security) if it involves an investment of money in a common enterprise with a reasonable expectation of profits to be derived from the efforts of others. This broad and flexible definition allows the SEC to regulate a wide array of financial transactions with the stated goal of protecting investors and maintaining fair and orderly functioning of the securities markets. However, many believe these protections are overreaching and even detrimental to the middle class attempting to create wealth. (You can hear more about this if you follow my friend and client A. J. Osborne.)

Once you have established that you are selling securities, what are your options? The first, as I mentioned, is an initial public offering (IPO). Think Microsoft or Facebook. In the entrepreneur world, these are fairly rare, so I won't spend a lot of time here. It involves registering the offering with the SEC, which has a ton of regulatory requirements, costs a lot of money, and takes a long time. This option can be good for companies that are readily scalable to a large market and have a unique value proposition, in addition to having a highly qualified leadership team. The second option is to find an exemption to the registration requirement. Most entrepreneurs find this exemption under Reg D, 506b, or 506c, although some looking to scale a little further use Reg CF (equity crowdfunding) or Reg A+ (like a mini-IPO). Most of my clients fall under Reg D, but some of the larger clients use Reg CF and Reg A+.

The third option: Your offering is illegal, and you are going to jail—well, maybe not jail, but it is illegal, even if you dress it up as a partnership and call it a JV. You don't actually decide whether what you are doing is a JV or selling securities; the facts determine that. So, if you don't like your circumstances, you can change your facts. Your qualified OPs will be knowledgeable enough about the rules to help you sort out where you can be flexible and where you need to be rigid. That's the beauty of having experts in your corner.

Reg D 506b allows you to accept up to 35 nonaccredited but sophisticated investors, *but* you cannot advertise or generally solicit, whereas Reg D 506c allows you to advertise and generally solicit (so long as your advertisements are not misleading). However, you may accept only accredited investors, *and* you must take reasonable steps to verify they are accredited before taking their money. (For a side-by-side comparison between 506b and 506c, see the handy chart in the appendix at the end.)

Awesome, so what is an accredited investor? For the most part, for now at least, an investor will qualify as accredited if they have had income above $200K for the previous two years and are reasonably expected to earn that again in the current year (or $300K if including a spouse), *or* if they have a net worth of more than $1M, excluding their primary residence. Otherwise, everyone who owns a home in California would qualify as accredited, even if they were otherwise broke. I kid, I kid—sort of. There are also certain licenses where one can qualify, but these are currently the main ways. There has been talk of increasing these income and net worth qualifications, and as of this writing, Congress is pressuring the SEC to allow a test whereby otherwise non-accredited investors could prove their knowledge and become an accredited investor without the income or net worth requirements.

There is a lot of debate about whether this is a good idea. If you've been paying attention, then you know that I am passionate about helping people create conscious wealth, regardless of their upbringing or the economic status they were born into. To require people to have a certain level of wealth to get access to the best investments maintains the status quo more than it protects would-be investors. Being wealthy, last I checked, does not necessarily equal being smart. And being poor or middle class does not mean less savvy or sophisticated. I recognize that there are other investment options for non-accredited investors, but they do not rise to the level of equal access. To offer deals to non-accredited investors, issuers of securities have to take on significant extra risk and expense, particularly if they intend to market to those investors. I was well into adulthood before I learned about any of this, so I would not have known anyone who could offer me an opportunity to invest in anything other than traditional stocks, which are not the best way to break out of the middle class in my opinion. The result is that the people with the best deals are incentivized to offer those deals only to accredited investors. Non-accredited investors are left with only two real options: 1) They either need to personally know someone offering an investment opportunity, or 2) They need to know where to find the few people offering investment opportunities through one of the more expensive routes I mentioned earlier, Reg CF or Reg A+.

This begs the question: Am I a proponent of allowing a testing option for investors not meeting income or net worth standards to qualify for accredited investor status? Not exactly. Hear me out. Let's say the SEC increases the annual income requirement to $500K and the net worth requirement to $10M. That eliminates most of the U.S. population from having access to arguably some of the best wealth-creating opportunities. Bring on the testing! Not so fast. Who is determining what knowledge and information make someone a suitable investor? Who is administering this test? Is it readily available to everyone everywhere at no cost? Is there an inherent bias in the test, as has been argued about every standardized test ever? A bunch of well-meaning people, along with a bunch of asshats who want to maintain the status quo to the detriment of anyone not like them, will probably argue and fight and hold up any meaningful delivery or application of said test. Why can we not let adults take personal responsibility for their choices, both good and bad, and decide, with the proper risk disclosures already required of those selling securities, and give them the choice to invest or not? A protectionist government, no matter how well-meaning, actually harms those it aims to protect. My two cents: I think we should allow general solicitation and advertising even when non-accredited investors are involved, and I think the laws in place governing those selling securities should apply equally, regardless of whether the investors are accredited. Wealthy people have been bamboozled by Ponzi schemes and fraudsters, too. Let's require the same level of disclosure and care of issuers, regardless of the financial status of investors.

If I haven't been canceled yet, let's move on to the other options, since the laws are still in place today. Crowdfunding has gained tremendous popularity in recent years as a means of raising OPM. Through online platforms, entrepreneurs can show-case their business ideas or products and invite contributions from many individuals. Crowdfunding is a general term that refers to the practice of raising funds from many individuals, typically through an online platform. It encompasses various forms of fundraising, including reward-based crowdfunding (offering incentives to backers), donation-based crowdfunding, and equity crowdfunding (offering shares in the company via Regulation Crowdfunding, or Reg CF). In reward-based crowdfunding, backers contribute funds for non-financial rewards or products. Donation-based crowdfunding involves collecting funds as donations without offering any specific rewards or products in return. Equity crowdfunding, on the other hand, allows individuals to invest in a company in exchange for equity or ownership shares. This approach not only raises capital but also creates a community of supporters. When issuing equity in the company through crowdfunding, there are a lot of regulations, so make sure you understand (and engage with OPs who understand) what your goals are and what you are getting into before you go this route.

Reg CF is a specific set of rules established by the SEC under the Jumpstart Our Business Startups (JOBS) Act. It allows small businesses and startups to raise funds through crowdfunding while complying with certain regulatory requirements. Reg CF provides a legal framework for equity crowdfunding, where businesses can sell securities to both accredited and non-accredited investors within specified limits. It sets limits on the amount that can be raised, imposes disclosure obligations, and requires the use of registered crowdfunding platforms.

To be clear, crowdfunding is a broader term encompassing various types of fundraising, while Reg CF is a specific regulatory framework for equity crowdfunding, providing guidelines and limitations for businesses looking to raise funds through this method. Using Reg CF as a method to raise capital offers several advantages and disadvantages for entrepreneurs. One significant advantage is the ability to raise funds from many individual investors, including non-accredited individuals. This democratized approach allows entrepreneurs to tap into a broader investor base and potentially generate more widespread support for their business. Reg CF also allows for easier online fundraising through crowdfunding platforms, simplifying the process of reaching potential investors and collecting funds. However, there are potential drawbacks to consider. The maximum amount that can be raised through Reg CF is limited, which may restrict the scalability of funding for larger projects or ambitious growth plans. Additionally, entrepreneurs must comply with strict regulatory requirements, including disclosure obligations and financial reporting, which can increase administrative burdens and costs. Furthermore, while Reg CF offers an opportunity to raise capital, there is no guarantee of success, and entrepreneurs must invest time and effort into marketing and promoting their offering to attract investors. Before you spend the money to hire those really solid OPs to help you with this, I would recommend talking to someone who has successfully used Reg CF as a method to raise capital and ask them for their experience relating to the limitations, costs, and legal considerations associated with it.

Much like Reg CF, using Reg A+ to raise capital also has its advantages and disadvantages. One major advantage is the ability to raise funds from both accredited and non-accredited investors, expanding your potential investor pool. This broader access to capital can be particularly beneficial for early-stage startups or businesses that may not meet the strict requirements of traditional fundraising avenues. Additionally, Reg A+ allows for greater flexibility than Reg D 506b in marketing and advertising the offering, enabling entrepreneurs to reach a wider audience and generate more interest in their business. However, there are major drawbacks to consider. The regulatory and compliance requirements for Reg A+ offerings are more complex and time-consuming compared to other fundraising methods. Entrepreneurs must navigate the rigorous filing and reporting processes, which can even further increase operational and administrative burdens and expenses. And while Reg A+ offers a streamlined review process by the SEC as compared to an IPO, there is still a level of scrutiny and due diligence that may result in delays or additional requirements. You should carefully evaluate the costs, time commitment, and legal implications associated with using Reg A+ before deciding to raise capital through this method.

I would be remiss if I did not mention there are a ton of resources to gain the education you need regarding OPM, as well as resources to gain access to opportunities—two of the three elements of creating conscious wealth. There is even an entire community of real estate investors focused on creative finance, which teaches people to create wealth without using their own money or credit. While he didn't invent creative finance, my friend and client Pace Morby, has created an enviable community of people who have created varying levels of wealth following his methods. Two of his focus areas are seller financing and "subject to" or "sub to." Seller financing is where, instead of going to a mortgage lender, bank, or private money lender, you ask the seller of whatever you are interested in buying if they will accept payments instead of all the cash up front. This can be a tremendous way to acquire real estate or a business without the typical hassles of going to a bank. A seller may be more motivated to give you a good deal because they have a vested interest in the deal happening. Subject to is where you can acquire real estate subject to the existing mortgage, taking over the payments from the seller. There are some regulatory requirements and potential risks to consider, but these options have worked for a lot of people as a creative way to leverage OPM.

Effectively leveraging OPM is a crucial strategy for entrepreneurs looking to scale their businesses rapidly. By understanding the various types of OPM available, you can identify the most suitable options for your specific needs. Each source of OPM comes with its own advantages and requirements, so you must carefully consider your goals, business model, and growth strategy.

The Best Way to Attract OPM

While it can be a bit scary and requires a bit of work, outside capital is an essential part of scaling almost any business. Now that you know the options for leveraging OPM, how do you get it? Attracting OPM can provide the necessary funding to take your business to the next level, and it is as much an art as it is a science. Every lane includes some manner of selling, so we might as well embrace that and learn to be good at it in a way that highlights our unique gifts and talents.

Investors and lenders want to know their money is going towards a well-thought-out business plan. Creating a strong business plan that outlines your goals, market analysis, and financial projections is essential to attract OPM. This doesn't necessarily mean an 80-page MBA-level business plan. Sometimes it can mean a 10-slide PowerPoint pitch deck. Depending on the business you are in, you should research what is appropriate. Regardless of the medium or format, your business plan should demonstrate that you have intentionally and consciously decided the direction you want to head, how the investment or loan will get you there, how the business will get the investor or lender whatever you projected in exchange for their loan or investment, and anything else that would be relevant to someone giving over their money for you to fund your dream. Pro tip: This should focus more on what the business will deliver to the world and why the lender or investor should care. Any pitch should focus on the opportunity and not on you. Additionally, remember your lane and your OPs, even here. Just because every lane includes some manner of sales, it still does not mean you should veer outside your lane to create a business plan. Lend your expertise where it makes sense and get help for the rest.

Investors and lenders want to know you are knowledgeable and experienced in your industry. This is one more place where bragging is encouraged, to a degree. This is not the time to be coy or humble, but be mindful of hubris. Demonstrating your expertise through case studies, industry recognition, or testimonials can help attract OPM without coming off as arrogant. Once again, your OPs come in clutch. Because you have surrounded yourself with only the best, let them brag for you. Pace Morby, the creative finance guy mentioned earlier, is a master at this. He has a way of engaging people who know him, and he asks them questions in a way that demonstrates his own expertise. He will have a student who he knows made a lot of money following his advice in the audience, call on that student and ask, "What have you learned on my coaching calls that you have applied to your investment business?" Because you have integrity, you're an expert in your field, and you'd do the same for them, your OPs will be happy to gush about you, too.

Sorry introverts, but networking is crucial in attracting OPM. Attend industry events, join relevant groups, and connect with professionals in your field. Building genuine connections can lead to investment opportunities. I am a huge proponent of in-person events because there is something so powerful about human connection (see Chapter 7 on Other People's Wisdom for more on this). Still, social media can be an excellent tool to an extent. LinkedIn and even Facebook are excellent ways to interact with people and begin to develop those meaningful connections. It is less about promoting yourself and more about engagement. A few people I know who are simply amazing at this are my former law partner Mauricio Rauld, the cost segregation king Yonah Weiss, and multifamily investor Amy Sylvis. They are each masters at posting content that is valuable to their followers, engaging and helping those followers, and promoting others. They don't need to aggressively sell their services or offerings because people know what they do by engaging with them in a meaningful way. Be like them, and people will be drawn to doing business with you.

One more sure-fire way to attract OPM is, you guessed it, to have the best OPs. Most people who lend or invest or buy or know anything about business will tell you that the success of a business is more about the team than literally anything else. Not the product or service. Not the economic climate. Not the money you have already invested. It is a stellar team. An A-team can turn a mediocre idea, property, or product into a winner by being creative, tenacious, smart, decisive, and cohesive as a team. This is one reason I say OPM is not enough to create wealth. To get that OPM, you need to be freed up to be your amazing self, and you need those OPs to shine as well.

Practicing Safe SEC

Attracting OPM can be an effective way to scale your business, but it comes with risks. To ensure you take OPM in the safest way possible, it's essential to follow certain guidelines. Again, since my focus is primarily on private securities, that's the lens through which I'll guide you in the safest way to take OPM and protect both your investors and your business.

That detailed business plan that helped you attract the OPM can also help mitigate risk by providing a roadmap for your business. Make sure your plan outlines your goals, target market, financial projections, and contingency plans. It will also protect you if an investor or lender is unhappy with the returns or the performance of the business because you can show you followed your business plan to the extent that doing so was feasible given all the facts and circumstances. The business plan is important, regardless of the type of OPM you use.

Conduct thorough due diligence on your team *and* your investors. Because you always want to be the buyer, not the seller, come up with your criteria for all your OPs, including OPM, before accepting investments, loans, partners, or any other role that is vital to your business. Read that again. Once more. You need to have rules and standards not just for business partners, but for your sources of OPM and even your customers and clients. Why? Because you are not chasing money, you are creating wealth consciousness. And when money is obtained in a way that does not align with your higher purpose, your goals, or your ethical and moral standards, it will not serve you in the ways you want. Every single thing you do should be intentional. Once you have made your rules, conducting thorough due diligence on your entire team of OPs will help ensure they are qualified to invest in, lend to, or work in your business, and this is one of the best ways to reduce the risk of fraud or other issues.

You would think it goes without saying, but I have learned in my many years of both practicing law and running businesses that it does need to be said: Hire experienced legal, tax, and financial professionals. While you should understand the general legal and regulatory requirements of running your business and accepting OPM in its various forms, you do not need to be, nor can you ever be—without years of schooling and real-world experience—an expert in these areas. Enlisting the help of experienced legal and financial professionals can help you navigate the specific requirements of accepting investments or other forms of OPM. These professionals can also help ensure your contracts and agreements protect both your investors and your business.

Just like with all your other OPs, it's essential to set clear investment terms and expectations with your investors and lenders. This includes outlining the expected return on investment, any risks involved, and any limitations or restrictions on their investment. Clear communication at the beginning, while everyone is still friendly, is a must. Waiting until there is an issue and trying to resolve it without clear written guidance leaves far too much room for emotion and bad blood to muddy the waters. Similarly, maintaining transparency throughout the relationship, whatever it is, builds trust and reduces the risk of misunderstandings or disputes. Be upfront about your business' financial situation and communicate regularly with your investors, lenders, and partners.

Finally, knowing where you are headed is the surest way to actually get there. Having an exit strategy in place mitigates risk by providing a plan for the source of your OPM to exit their investment when appropriate. You set these terms up in advance, and you get to control this process with proper planning. This can include selling the company or buying back shares at a predetermined price or a myriad of other options. The general rule here is that you can do *almost* anything you want as long as you disclose it upfront, and you can sell it to investors, partners, and lenders.

Other People's Credit

In the journey of entrepreneurship, capital is more than currency; it's a catalyst for growth. But what if your financial resources or credit history don't measure up to your ambitions? This is where the power of Other People's Credit (OPC) becomes a game-changer.

OPC, at its core, involves using the creditworthiness of others to gain access to financial resources that might otherwise be inaccessible. This could mean partnering with someone who has a stronger credit score to secure a loan or finding investors who can offer credit endorsements or guarantees. The most obvious benefit is the increased access to funds. More capital can mean the difference between slow, organic growth and a rapid, strategic expansion. For new businesses, establishing credit can be a Catch-22. Leveraging OPC can help build your business credit score, making future financing easier and potentially cheaper. OPC can reduce personal risk as well. Instead of leveraging your personal credit, using OPC can help shield your personal finances from direct exposure.

Leveraging OPC can provide access to financing, which can help to fund the start or the growth of your business. It can increase your buying power, which can help to acquire assets or make investments that may have been otherwise unaffordable. It can help to reduce costs, as it eliminates the need to raise capital through other means, such as equity or debt offerings, or it can enhance these other means. Leveraging OPC can help to build relationships with lenders or investors, which can be beneficial in the long term. And, of course, using OPC can enhance your personal creditworthiness, making it easier to obtain financing for other ventures as well.

The ideal OPC partner should share your business vision. Trust and mutual benefit are key. As in any ethical transaction, you must be transparent about your intentions and the risks involved. Legal agreements that outline responsibilities and contingencies can save you a lot of heartache and misery if done in the beginning of any relationship. When you are aligned with business goals, you ensure both parties are working towards the same objectives.

Of course, you must borrow responsibly. The aim should be to use OPC to generate income that exceeds the cost of capital. Sound business decisions are even more important when you are working with someone else's credit, money, or other capital. Use OPC as a stepping stone to build your business's creditworthiness and financial history, and you will grow toward that big goal you've set even faster.

My client, John, has used this strategy better than anyone else I have seen. He's a really smart business person, great with numbers, and relates well with people. However, he went through a nasty divorce, which destroyed his financial situation and his credit. To build back his empire, John partnered with a like-minded friend Steve, also intelligent and savvy but needing some serious operational help to pursue his dreams of financial independence. Steve was not as good with the numbers, but he trusted John implicitly, *and* he had great credit. John found properties in which to invest and ran the numbers to make sure they could add enough value to make a hefty profit, while Steve signed on the loan and helped with other aspects of the business. The two created a sizable empire while John repaired his credit. Now, John can sign on the loans for others to help them build their own empires. He's a shining example of how to leverage OPC to exponentially grow your conscious wealth. And paying it forward is a testament to not only his integrity but to how much he believes in the power of OPE.

If you cannot directly partner with someone who lends their credit, there are advantages of having a key principal ("KP") with established relationships with lenders, investors, and industry professionals. You can give equity to someone who lends their credit and the corresponding relationships in a one-off transaction to help launch or expand your business.

As with any business relationship, you must always conduct due diligence and select a KP with a strong reputation and track record. Just because you feel like you need OPC does not mean you are beholden to anyone who offers it. Your reputation is on the line as well.

I caution you to enter into these relationships with your eyes wide open. The intersection of financial and personal relationships can be complex. Clear boundaries and written agreements are essential. Avoid becoming overly reliant on OPC. Like with John, the goal should be to eventually stand on your own financial footing and even offer the same support to someone else when you are able. Whenever dealing with such a delicate dynamic as personal credit and the exchange for other services, ensure that leveraging OPC does not cross into misuse or manipulation by either party. The trust your partner places in you is a valuable asset in itself.

OPC is a powerful tool, but it's most effective when viewed as a temporary bridge to greater financial independence. Used wisely and ethically, it can unlock doors that were previously closed, paving the way for your business's success and stability. Remember, the key to leveraging OPC is not just in the financial resources it brings but in the confidence it instills in yourself and your business. As you build a track record of success and responsibility, you're not just leveraging OPC but building your legacy.

Chapter 5
OPA
Other People's Assets

Other People's Homes

W e've covered a wide variety of opportunities to leverage OPM. Now, we turn the key to another door: the power of leveraging Other People's Homes. Times are changing, and this is a concept that is catching on.

We live in a world where the very concept of home has evolved beyond a mere dwelling place, and enterprising individuals have discovered the potential of leveraging Other People's Homes as a cornerstone for creating conscious wealth. Conscious wealth doesn't simply mean generating income but doing so in a way that respects community values and fosters sustainable growth. And doing so in a way that honors your loftiest goals for your magical life.

Imagine for a moment the multitude of homes that sit idle, the vacation properties that lay dormant for seasons, or the city apartments that await the return of their jet-setting owners. These underutilized spaces are brimming with potential, and with the right approach, they can be transformed into vessels of opportunity not only for their owners but also for the savvy entrepreneur.

The sharing economy has flung open the gates to these possibilities. Platforms such as Airbnb, VRBO, Peerspace, and others have made it possible to connect with homeowners who are looking to monetize their spaces without the commitment of traditional rental or sale. But it's not just about temporary stays; it's about creating experiences that guests will treasure, which elevates the value of the property and the community it nestles in.

For the conscious wealth creator, leveraging Other People's Homes means curating these spaces into more than just places to sleep. It's about creating a homey atmosphere, a unique experience, and a connection to the local culture. It's hosting workshops, retreats, or pop-up events that enrich both the guests and the neighborhood. It's finding the intersection where hospitality meets impact.

But how does one walk this path with integrity and success? Well, I have some ideas on the subject. Work with local artisans, chefs, and guides to create authentic experiences that also support the local economy. Implement eco-friendly measures within the home, from recycling programs to green energy sources, ensuring that your business footprint is as light as the linen on the beds. When promoting these homes, do so with a narrative that respects the homeowners' stories and the community's culture, ensuring that the marketing is as much about storytelling as it is about selling. Focus on providing quality experiences rather than just increasing the number of bookings. A well-curated stay can command a higher value and create repeat guests. Navigate the regulations of short-term rentals with diligence and respect. Ensure that all operations are legal and ethical and contribute positively to the community.

The result? A mutually beneficial ecosystem where home-owners generate income from their otherwise unused properties, guests enjoy unique and enriching experiences, and the local community thrives from increased economic activity and cultural exchange. Leveraging Other People's Homes in this manner is not about exploitation; it's about partnership and creativity. It's about recognizing the hidden value in empty spaces and transforming them into hubs of cultural and economic vitality.

It's an opportunity to craft a business that not only fills your pockets but also fills homes with life, neighborhoods with growth, and guests with unforgettable memories. This, in essence, is the heart of conscious capitalism—where profit meets purpose and where the homes of today become the heritage of tomorrow. Entire communities are popping up around this concept. Third Home and others have figured out that luxury doesn't have to mean hoarding all the good stuff just for yourself.

A few of my incredible guests on my show, *Bubbles with Bethany,* where we have conversations with successful and inspiring guests about conscious capitalism, have this dialed in to a tee. Rob Abasolo and Avery Carl are two pros in the short-term rental space. They teach people how to create success in this arena, but they also create unique experiences for their guests.

The focus is on the strategic and mindful approach to lever-aging real estate as an asset for creating wealth that benefits both the individual and the community. When we emphasize the importance of sustainability, authenticity, and legal compliance in the pursuit of wealth through collaborative consumption, we can positively impact all involved. And who doesn't love a win-win?

Other People's Real Estate

Real estate has long stood as a bastion of wealth creation, a tangible asset that, unlike the ephemeral stock ticker, you can see, touch, and improve upon. Yet, the barriers to entry can be high, and the risks can be significant. That is unless you have the right OPs. This is where the leveraging of OPRE shines as a strategy for those visionaries looking to expand their influence and construct their empire with no need for massive capital investment.

Envision a world where the real estate you utilize to grow your enterprise isn't yours by deed but by strategy. I'm not talking about the mere acquisition of property; I'm talking about the innovative use of existing spaces to create value and generate wealth.

Consider the entrepreneur who, rather than purchasing office space, utilizes coworking environments to house their operations, taking advantage of built-in networking opportunities and flexible lease terms. Or the restaurateur who finds success not by constructing new buildings but by transforming existing spaces through pop-up culinary experiences that captivate an audience with a taste for the novel and exclusive.

The power of leveraging OPRE lies in the strategic partnership with property owners. For the property owner, it's the optimization of their investment, and for the entrepreneur, it's the stage upon which their empire will rise. It's a symbiosis where underutilized spaces become the ground upon which new ventures flourish. You may have guessed that real estate is my favorite tool for creating conscious wealth, but it doesn't always have to look like a typical real estate sales transaction. If you take nothing else from this book, remember the ideas of community, collaboration, co-creation, and creativity. That's a lot of Cs.

What do I mean by this? Get creative. Engage in lease agreements that allow for the shared use of space, reducing overhead while fostering a community of complementary businesses. Look for opportunities to activate unused spaces in ways that benefit both the property owner and the business owner, like hosting events or offering business services. In an economy where the traditional office model is evolving, offer flexible workspaces that cater to the modern entrepreneur's need for agility and adaptability. Use short-term rental platforms to host temporary retail or hospitality ventures, thereby testing markets without the commitment of a long lease. Sublease a part of a larger property for your business, ensuring that your presence adds value to the primary tenant's business as well.

By leveraging OPRE, you can swiftly scale your operations, adapt to market demands, and avoid the financial burdens that often accompany solo property ownership. This approach can significantly reduce the risk profile of your ventures and provide a runway for rapid experimentation and innovation.

Yet, as with all aspects of OPE, leveraging real estate demands a keen sense of responsibility. It requires a commitment to maintaining strong relationships with the other property owners, respect for the spaces you occupy, and a dedication to leaving a positive mark on the physical and community landscape.

OPRE is not just a means to an end but a cornerstone of an entrepreneurial empire. It's a testament to the idea that the most enduring empires are built not solely through ownership but through vision, collaboration, and the strategic utilization of the resources at hand.

Another option is through JVs, when two or more people pool their resources and expertise to invest in a property they co-own. This can be a great way to share the risks and rewards of real estate investing, and it allows you to tap into Other People's Knowledge and Experience. If you're just starting out, you may not have the capital to buy your own property, but you can still use Other People's Property to build your business.

Finally, you can also leverage OPRE through partnerships and collaborations. For example, you could team up with a property owner to develop or renovate a property, or you could partner with a real estate agent to find and negotiate deals.

When you search for it, you'll find there are many ways to leverage OPRE to build wealth and grow your business. By tapping into Other People's Knowledge, Expertise, and Resources, you can achieve your goals more quickly and efficiently.

Other People's Deals

The power of Other People's Deals is not about crafting deals from scratch but rather the artistry of leveraging existing ones as a potent strategy for amplifying business growth. In your life as an entrepreneur, your days are filled with the pursuit of deals that will propel your business forward. But pause for a moment and consider the untapped potential that lies in the deals already set in motion by others. This could mean anything from JVs and affiliate partnerships to tapping into the expansive networks and audiences others have cultivated.

By aligning with other businesses, you unlock doors to their customer bases, inviting new prospects into your fold. Partnering opens a window to increased exposure, casting the spotlight on your brand and drawing the eyes of potential clients or customers. There's also the allure of shared risk, as collaboration dilutes the inherent dangers of business ventures. And perhaps most enticing is the prospect of new revenue streams flowing into your business with a fraction of the investment in time and resources typically required.

To navigate this landscape effectively, start by identifying businesses that complement your own. These symbiotic relationships ensure that any joint endeavor is mutually beneficial. Clarity in your objectives is crucial; knowing what you aim to achieve and what you can offer is the cornerstone of successful partnerships. Creativity is your ally here—don't shy away from unconventional ideas that could prove to be fruitful. And above all, communication is paramount; clear, transparent dialogue is the bedrock of solid business relationships.

Other People's Data

Consider the entrepreneur who realizes the mutual benefits of affiliate marketing, promoting another's products to a receptive audience, or the visionary who forges a JV, creating a product that blends the strengths of two entities. Guest hosting podcasts, too, serves as a vessel for expanding your brand's reach, and sponsorships can introduce your offerings to a fresh cadre of potential customers.

Embracing Other People's Data is not just about business expansion; it's about smart, strategic growth. It's about building bridges rather than islands, about reaching further by standing on the platforms others have constructed. Remember, the right partnerships and collaborations can propel your business into new realms of success.

Leveraging one's following or email list to assist Other People with their deals in exchange for some form of compensation is also common. As we dive further into the digital sphere, influencers and affiliate marketers find themselves in a dance with legality and ethics. Nerd lawyer alert: The Federal Trade Commission in the United States mandates clear disclosure of paid promotions. Every tweet, post, or story must bear the truth of its origins —whether it's compensation, affiliation, or partnership. The advertising must be honest, and the endorsements must be grounded in genuine experience. And when it comes to monetizing contact lists, consent is king. The law requires clarity and transparency with those whose details you hold. Platforms that facilitate the sharing of such lists must be vetted for their adherence to regulations and their commitment to user privacy. Every individual must have the power to step back and opt out, should they choose to sever the tie that binds them to the third-party marketer.

If you have a large contact list, you may have considered monetizing it by selling or renting it out to third-party marketers. However, it's important to understand the legal considerations involved in this type of activity. Before you can share your contact list with third-party marketers, you need to obtain explicit consent from each individual on your list. This can be done through a consent form or by having individuals opt in to your email list. You also need to provide a clear explanation of how their information will be used and who it will be shared with. Depending on where you live, there may be data protection laws that govern how contact lists can be used and shared. Make sure you are familiar with any applicable laws and that you are complying with them. If you're going to rent or sell your contact list, it's important to use a reputable platform that has a track record of protecting user data and complying with relevant laws and regulations. There are several platforms available, such as UpLead and Lead411, that offer list rental and sales services. It's important to be transparent with your audience about your intentions for sharing their information. Let them know you are planning to rent or sell their information to third-party marketers and provide them with a clear explanation of how their information will be used. It's also important to provide individuals on your contact list with the option to opt out of having their information shared with third-party marketers. This can be done through an unsubscribe link in your emails or by providing a clear way for individuals to request their information be removed from your list.

By following these guidelines, you can get paid to share your contact list legally and ethically. However, it's important to remember your reputation is on the line, so make sure you are only sharing your list with reputable marketers and you are transparent with your audience about your intentions.

Leveraging Other People's Data represents a pathway to growth that is rich with potential if the rules that govern it and the ethical considerations it entails are respected. It's a testament to the notion that in the world of business, sometimes the most fruitful ventures are those that are shared.

Chapter 6
OPT
Other People's Time and Talents

Other People's Time

As a business owner, your time is one of your most valuable resources. And, there is only so much you can get done on your own. If you want to scale your business, you will need to leverage the time of OP.

One of the primary benefits of using Other People's Time is that it allows you to focus on your core competencies. Now that you have identified what your lane is, of course you need to free up your time so you may be free to focus only on your lane. The biggest excuse I hear from business owners is that they don't have enough time. I'm guilty of it myself if my OPs aren't reminding me. You don't have enough time because you have not specifically declared what is worthy of your time and what is not. As a business owner, there are certain tasks that only you can do. However, there are many other tasks that can be delegated to others. By outsourcing these tasks, you can free up your time to focus on what you do best. Like most things that sound awesome (if not a little trite), it is easier said than done. I get it. But the most important thing you will do in your life is to truly hand over what is eating into your precious time. After all, isn't that one of the big three freedoms? Time, location, and financial.

A tool I came up with in one of my one-on-one coaching sessions is what I call my "Absofuckinglutely Analyzer." I had seen a post where Main Street business influencer Codie Sanchez gave away the deal analyzer that she uses to determine whether she will buy a particular business. She set her parameters, and every deal had to meet those parameters, or she would not buy it. It took the emotion out of decision-making. I decided I needed a deal analyzer for my life. I was spending too much time on stuff I either didn't want to be doing or that took me away from, rather than propelling me closer to, my ultimate vision. Now, I know I already told you that I defined my lane to avoid doing things that I am not both amazing at and that light me up. But even though I have defined my lane, stuff creeps in. It may look like my lane at first glance, or it may be just shiny enough that I want to veer toward those lane lines to check it out. But give me a break; I'm human too.

So I occasionally fall back into my "I'm too busy" nonsense. I know when I am getting off track because I start canceling my standing coaching meetings where the sole focus is on me and my mindset and how I will reach my ultimate vision. I ask you if there is a more important meeting (other than with my daughter). There isn't. Not one. Recently, this very thing happened. I have a lot going on, just like you do, and I got wrapped up in the details of things, and I got weighed down by all the opportunity. You may be thinking, *Oh, poor you, with all your opportunity,* but I am merely making the point that sometimes, even when there is a ton of amazing stuff coming at me, it can be overwhelming to decide where to focus my energy. Articulating my ultimate vision and defining my lane have helped me determine where I spend my efforts, time, and money, but sometimes things pop up that may be disguised as something that gets me closer but is really a distraction. Distractions are not our friends, and we want to avoid them at all costs. So to further distill the direction of my energy and my focus, I present to you the Absofuckinglutely Analyzer. It is my personal checklist of how I determine whether something that demands my time, in fact, gets it. There are the big things, the rocks, that are easy. But those pesky little tasks that may seem simple or innocuous enough need to be analyzed based on predetermined sets of criteria and not in-the-moment emotion. Sadly, I am a recovering people pleaser, and when asked by someone to do something, my gut reaction is to try to find a way to do it, not to determine whether I *should*.

The general idea behind the Absofuckinglutely Analyzer is that if something, once gone through my checklist, is not an enthusiastic yes, then it has to be a no. I need an OP to do it, or maybe it just doesn't get done. You've heard it before: automate, delegate, or eliminate. Because I am so clear on what my vision is for my life, and I know what I am awesome at, and I know what really gets me going, it's easier to determine how to further filter each little potentially time-wasting thing. Don't get me wrong. It will take practice creating your own analyzer (you may choose to call it something else—this name just spoke to me), but also not doing the things that don't make it through. These are the things that don't get you closer to your dream life. They are stealing the one thing you can never recover: your time.

Another clear benefit of using Other People's Time is that it allows you to scale your business. In case you haven't been paying attention, one of my passions, and a big part of my lane, is helping you scale your business along with your wealth and your magical life experiences. I cannot emphasize enough that reclaiming your time is critical. When you're just starting out, you may be able to handle everything on your own—and you may have to for a while. However, as your business grows, you will absolutely need to hire additional staff or contractors to help you manage the workload. By using Other People's Time, you can build a team of skilled professionals who can help you take your business to the next level.

So, how can you effectively use Other People's Time to your advantage? Creating your own Absofuckinglutely Analyzer should include some basic filters, and then I want you to really dig deep to fine-tune it so that eventually, with some time and practice, you have created a life for yourself where every single thing you do brings you joy. The lawyer in me feels compelled to state that I am not saying you will never have hardships, your life will be perfect, or bad things won't happen. However, you can always choose how you respond to all such things. And the analyzer can help.

Everything that takes my time and energy must move me closer to my extraordinary life. If it does not, then I need to pass on it. This includes my relationships. If someone is not part of my growth, then I have to limit their access to me. All love and respect, but from afar. OK, so here it is. Feel free to use it exactly as it is or change it to suit your own needs.

The Absofuckinglutely Analyzer Checklist:

Determining the Worthiness of a Task or Opportunity

1. Alignment with Ultimate Vision

Direct Contribution: Does it significantly contribute to short-term and long-term objectives?
Consistency with Values: Is it in harmony with my core values and principles?

2. Time and Resource Commitment

Time-Efficiency: Can it be accomplished within a reasonable time frame?

Resource Availability: Do I have (or can easily get) the resources needed without straining current commitments?

3. Financial Assessment

Profit Potential: Does it offer a tangible and satisfactory financial return?

Budget Alignment: Can it be accomplished within my current or adjustable budget?

Risk Mitigation: Have I identified potential financial risks and developed mitigation strategies?

4. Skills and Expertise

Competency: Do I possess the requisite skills and knowledge?

Skill Enhancement: Will it significantly enhance my skills or knowledge in a beneficial area?

5. Network and Relationship Building

Strategic Connections: Does it open doors to valuable networks or partnerships?

Reputation Enhancement: Will it positively impact my personal or business reputation?

6. Personal Satisfaction and Wellness

Joy and Passion: Does it resonate with what I enjoy or am passionate about?
Well-Being: Can it be pursued without compromising mental and physical health?

7. Impact and Legacy

Positive Impact: Does it have the potential to create a positive change in the community or industry?
Legacy Building: Does it contribute toward leaving a meaningful legacy?

8. Opportunity Cost

Best Use of Time: Is this the best possible use of my time and resources at the moment?
Alternative Opportunities: Have I considered and evaluated alternative options and their potential?

9. Exit and Adaptation Strategy

Pivot Potential: Can it be adapted or modified if initial plans don't pan out?
Exit Strategy: Is there a clear and manageable strategy for ending the commitment if necessary?

10. Legal and Ethical Compliance

Legality: Does it adhere to all applicable laws and regulations?

Ethical Soundness: Is it in alignment with ethical considerations and guidelines?

Final Assessment:

Absolute Alignment: Does it align deeply and broadly with multiple criteria mentioned above?

Note: An enthusiastic YES should ideally mean that the task or opportunity aligns with a substantial majority of the above criteria. If it meets only a few, or if it strongly misaligns with even one critical criterion, it may be worth reconsidering or further evaluating the task or opportunity.

Download your own
Absofuckinglutely Analyzer
to help you determine
the worthiness of a
task or opportunity.

SCAN THE QR CODE

Using this analyzer, you should be able to assess opportunities or tasks with a more structured, objective lens, ensuring they align not just with immediate needs but also with your broader, long-term vision and objectives. Adjust criteria as per your unique contexts and goals for better-fitting assessments. Always consider seeking advice from your OPs, your mentors, or advisors for large-scale opportunities or tasks.

Other kinds of things you want to consider as you determine if something is going to be an undue strain on your time:

- Is this a non-core task? Identify tasks that are important but not central to your business or central to launching you closer to your ultimate vision, such as bookkeeping, graphic design, or social media management. These tasks can be outsourced to contractors or virtual assistants who have the expertise to handle them efficiently and effectively.
- Does this non-core task require more than a virtual assistant or contractor? If you need more hands-on support, consider hiring employees to help you manage your business. This could include salespeople, customer service representatives, or administrative staff. If you are like me and hiring isn't your core competency and is outside your lane, this is one area I give you a pass to at least get good at it for one really good hire and then let that person hire the rest of your OPs according to your ultimate vision and business plan.
- Could this task or opportunity be better suited as a collaboration with other businesses rather than something you need to tackle on your own? Look for opportunities to collaborate with other businesses that have complementary skills and expertise. For example, if you run a marketing agency, you could partner with a web design company to offer a more comprehensive suite of services to your clients.

- Could this task be automated? Automation tools can help you streamline your business processes and save time. For example, you can use email marketing software to automate your email campaigns or project management tools to keep your team organized. And don't even get me started on the amazingness that is AI!
- How can you help your OPs get this done for you if it does not meet the criteria in the analyzer? Invest in training. If you have employees or contractors, invest in training to help them develop the skills they need to perform their jobs effectively. This will not only improve their performance but also free up your time to focus on other tasks.

Time freedom is the freedom that buys you all other freedoms. Controlling your time is the best way to leverage it. Mike Downey, a passive investor in my LinkedIn network, posted the following relating to a study he conducted on time management, which I found enlightening.

Here's how people say time management helped them:
91 percent say it reduces stress
90 percent increases productivity
86 percent improved focus on tasks
84 percent reach goals faster
83 percent better decision-making
82 percent increases confidence
75 percent better relationships
73 percent say it leads to *more* time

For him, this meant MORE time for his family and BEING MORE PRESENT for his kids. His response to this was to throw out the old TO-DO list and begin TIME BLOCKING. I don't know if that rings true for you or not, but I know you can certainly significantly reduce your TO-DO list by leveraging Other People's Time and then attack what's left using whichever method works for you.

To achieve success, leveraging Other People's Time can be a game-changer. Whether you're an entrepreneur, a student, or a busy professional, using Other People's Time can help you to maximize your productivity, freeing up time to focus on the things that get through your analyzer. You can actually learn new skills when you work with Other People because you can learn from their experiences and expertise. This can help you develop new skills and expand your knowledge base, which can be invaluable for achieving success. You obviously increase your capacity when you have Other People's Time working for you. When you work alone, your capacity is limited by your own time and energy. But when you leverage Other People's Time, you can increase your capacity and take on more projects or clients. Working with others can help you build stronger relationships and develop a network of people who can support you in your goals. This can be invaluable for achieving success and advancing your career. It's always a goal to achieve a greater work-life balance (and by that, I really just mean spending more time on the things that matter most to you, whether that's family, friends, hobbies, personal growth, or doing the things within your lane that help you achieve conscious wealth).

Whether you're delegating tasks, working with a mentor, or collaborating with colleagues, there are many ways to leverage Other People's Time to achieve your goals. So don't be afraid to ask for help, and remember that success is often a team effort!

Other People's Talents

It's also critical you leverage Other People's Talents. To attract the best talent, you should have already identified your own unique gifts and talents. I know I keep saying this, but it is so important that it bears repeating. And this one seems the simplest to me. We all have gifts and talents. Whether we recognize what they are yet is another story (see Chapter 7 on Other People's Wisdom for some tips on how to recognize yours if you haven't already).

As a business owner, you are probably trying to do everything yourself. After all, that is the hallmark of a true entrepreneur, isn't it? The ability and desire to roll up our sleeves and get done whatever needs to be done. At least when we get started and before we learn to harness the power of OPE. However, continuing to do everything yourself can be a recipe for burnout and, ultimately, failure. But now you know what is, and equally important, what is *not* your lane. Which talents are necessary for you to succeed that are not your skill set? Who do you know that is amazing at that thing? Are they already in your network? If not, leverage Other People's Networks (see Chapter 9). Are you seeing the patterns yet? There is an OP for literally everything you need, and you are less than six degrees of separation away from it at any given moment. Kevin Bacon's got nothing on you!

You already know that by building a team of talented individuals and leveraging their strengths, you can achieve greater success than you ever could alone. You already know that you can increase efficiency and productivity by delegating tasks to individuals with the right skills and expertise. You already know that the quality of your output will be better with a diverse set of talents and skills on your team versus going it alone. You even know that by leveraging Other People's Talents, you can tap into new ideas and perspectives that you might not have thought of on your own, which will probably lead to increased innovation and growth for your business. You probably also know that when you have a team of talented individuals with diverse backgrounds and experiences, you can make better decisions that are informed by a variety of perspectives. So why haven't you done it? Perhaps you don't know where to start. Perhaps you need a mindset shift. Let's fix that, shall we?

Here are a few ways to leverage Other People's Talents to benefit your business. When you're building your team, focus on hiring individuals with diverse talents and expertise that complement your own, not mirror your own. Look for individuals who bring unique perspectives and experiences to the table. Do not go and find more of you. You will be tempted. You will see yourself looking back at you, and you will want to, with all of your being, say, "YES! *This* person really gets me. This person will take care of my business as I would. This is who I need in my life!" That's your ego talking. That's familiarity. You ever heard the phrase "get comfortable being uncomfortable?" That applies here. You do not need another you. You need someone whose values align with your own. You need someone whose goals are aligned with what you need them to do. But they do not need to have the same goals you have. In fact, I would argue they should have slightly different goals that can be satisfied by doing whatever it is you need done. For example, my head of operations is vastly different than I am. She wants to lead a team of amazing and talented people to build a successful company. She wants to build it. She does not want to dream it up. She does not want to be the face of it. She does not want to generate new and exciting ideas, markets, partners, products, or solutions. That's my job. She wants to create an environment where I can do all those things, and she can make sure all of our OPs get them done. I adore her. She and I share many of the same beliefs about how a company should be run, what the culture should feel like, and what we want to embody as an ethos. But she is awesome in many of the things that are not my strengths. And I am awesome at things she simply does not want to do. It's perfect. OK, maybe not perfect, as no relationship is perfect, but we enjoy each other, and we respect each other, and we trust each other enough to be real and honest with each other, even when it may be uncomfortable.

Once you have your team in place, assign tasks based on each individual's strengths and expertise, not just on what needs to be done at the moment. Your OPs will achieve greater efficiency and higher-quality results if you really let them shine in their own lanes. Plus, if you want them to stick around, this is the only way to go. Just as you don't want to do things you don't enjoy for very long, neither do they. Scaling means creating sustainability, and happy OPs are the only way to do that while also creating a happy and healthy company culture.

Encourage your team to work together and collaborate. When you foster an environment of teamwork, you open the door to fresh ideas and different perspectives, which can drive innovation and fuel growth for your business. The days of creating a competitive environment within an organization are fading, and that death cannot happen soon enough if you ask me. Pitting people against each other creates animosity and silos within an organization, and while it may produce some short-term wins, that will fizzle out, and only the most cutthroat will survive. I don't know about you, but that is not an environment I want to create.

One of my favorite clients and favorite people, Ashley Wilson of Bar Down Investments and Conference Connect, and author of *The Only Woman in the Room,* gave some advice to an audience of real estate entrepreneurs that has stuck with me over the years. Ashley advises that when we seek to leverage the talents of others, we should LEAD WITH OUR STRENGTHS. When you are seeking partners, team members, investors, or any other talent you need, tell those prospective talent bringers what you bring to the table. How can *you* help *them?* Ashley lives by the phrase, "Give more than you get, and you will get all you need."

When you offer to share your unique gifts and talents with others, you are doing a couple of important things. First, you are reinforcing your value in your own mind, and we have already established that MINDSET is critical to success. Second, you are coming from a position of strength and making others feel more open to collaborating by sharing how you can help them rather than putting a burden on them. For example, if you are looking for investors, do not tell them you need $25M so you can acquire a property and fix it up. Tell them you are raising capital to add a projected $10M in value to an already cash-flowing property by adding a pool, fixing the roof, and improving the marketing plan. Then, you plan to refinance and get the investors a healthy return. You plan to offer an eight percent preferred return and an equity split of 80 percent of net profit. This is offering one of those three elements of conscious wealth we discussed: access to opportunities.

Do not tell a prospective partner you need someone to help you with asset management because you don't have any experience. Tell them you are an expert underwriter and you are the best in the business at sourcing deals. Whatever it is you do, just make sure it is true, and you can back it up.

When you look for a job, you don't go into an interview saying, "Hey, I need money to support my coffee habit and to take care of these kids." While that may be true, you say, "I have excellent communication skills and work well under pressure." Why would you not do that in all areas of life? You know what you've got— flaunt it!

And when you lead with your strengths, you will have solidified what your lane is. And in so doing, you should have determined what it is not. Stay in your lane. Be the best of the best in that lane. And do whatever you can to find and attract the best of the best in those lanes that are not yours.

When my clients hire me to be their lawyer, they are not hiring me because I already know all the answers to all their questions. They hire me because my particular expertise allows me to know how to find the answers they need and, this is the most important part, to know which information is relevant to answer the question in the context that matters to the client. Anyone can ask Google or Siri or Alexa or ChatGPT or whatever other magic box literally anything they want. There is no shortage of information or access to it. I would argue that there is too much access to too much information for it all to be meaningful and digestible. And so, clients hire me because I know how to weed out irrelevant or extraneous information and use the rest to explain difficult legal concepts to them in a way that makes sense and that they can use in their business. They hire me to provide them with security so that when they go out and raise OPM, they are doing so safely and legally (practicing safe SEC). They hire me because I make them feel comfortable in an otherwise uncomfortable space. My talent is trusted advisor, counselor, mage. Did that seem like a brag? You're goddamn right it is. Have you not been paying attention? We do that now.

At the same time, I suck at keeping house. I hate it; it takes me way longer than is reasonable for the task that it is, and it takes me away from other things that I enjoy more and that I am better at doing. Remember back when my inner goddess would make requests of me, and I would shut her down? This is one instance where she got her way fairly early on. She used to think that achieving success meant hiring someone to clean the house. So the minute I could, I did. It was hard at first because I was worried people would think I was being precious or that I would seem entitled. I justified myself at every opportunity: *I work too much and just don't have time. I gave up another luxury to have this one. I still clean most of the time; this is just for the heavy-duty deep cleaning.*

First of all, who in the actual fuck cares whether I pay to have my house cleaned? No one is thinking that much about me or how I spend my money. And if they are, why do I care? Are they cleaning my house? But evidently, I had one of those pesky deep-seated beliefs about what it means to pay people to do things I am capable of doing myself. I don't have that issue when I pay to have my oil changed or my hair done. So why this? Who makes up these rules? I will tell you who. I do, for me. And you do, for you.

And I'll do you one better. Not only does paying someone to do these things for me (that I am perfectly capable of doing but hate) reduce my stress, I make more money by handing it off. And I don't just mean my hourly wage is more than theirs because I don't want that to be the measuring stick. It's not that transactional. I mean that I have freed up creative space and energy to imagine new ways to use my gifts and talents to build my empire, many of which make me more money. I used to feel like I had to be working on something billable every minute a cleaner was working in my house to prove (to whom I do not know) that it was justified to have them clean. Now, I do whatever I want because that is the point of all of this! Do we sometimes have to do things we don't want to do to be successful? Of course. I am not suggesting we don't work hard or pay our dues; I am simply stating we should really minimize how much time we spend there and find OP Talents as quickly as we can. And we should be working hard only on things that matter to us.

I have recently seen an influencer client of mine talking about how he hired a private chef because it saves him money. Between planning the meals, going to the grocery store, unloading the groceries, preparing the meals, and cleaning up, he was spending so much time, energy, and mental capacity doing something he did not enjoy, which was taking time away from his family. Once he really netted it out, it made no sense *not* to hire a chef. This may not be true of everyone, and I recognize that everyone reading this may not yet be able to afford a cleaner or a private chef. But I truly believe if you put all the tips in this book (and others I have mentioned throughout) into practice, you will find a way to put Other People's Talents to work for you. If we get away from the idea that it is a luxury to have someone help us by doing what they are amazing at so that we can spend time doing what we are amazing at, we can shift the mindset to where it becomes necessary to build our empires to seek out Other People's Talents. We all find ways to get our necessities. We just need to reframe it.

Chapter 7
OPB
Other People's Brains

Using Other People's Ideas (OPI) and Other People's Intellectual Property (OPIP) are two different concepts with distinct legal implications. Using someone else's ideas involves taking inspiration from their concepts or general direction without necessarily replicating any specific elements of their work. For example, an entrepreneur might attend a conference and hear about a new business idea they find interesting and then go on to develop their own version of that idea that is unique to them. In this case, they are not necessarily infringing on anyone's IP, but are instead using Other People's Ideas to spark their own creativity.

On the other hand, using someone else's IP involves using specific elements of their work that are protected by law, such as trademarks, copyrights, or patents. This can include copying a product design, using copyrighted images or text without permission, or selling a product that infringes on someone else's patent.

In general, it is legal to use Other People's Ideas as inspiration, but it is not legal to use their IP without permission. If you are unsure about whether you are infringing on someone's IP, it is always best to ask or seek legal advice to avoid potential legal disputes. So, why am I suggesting you use Other People's IP? Because if done properly and legally, it's a damn good way to achieve your goals more quickly.

Using Other People's Ideas and Intellectual Property can be a great way to spark innovation. By taking existing concepts and putting your own spin on them, you can create something unique and valuable. Have you ever been listening to a podcast or a fantastic interview and had a genius idea pop into your head based on something they said? Have you ever read a book that had such a profound impact on you that you took those concepts and ran with them to build your empire? Yeah, I'm fishing. Just go with it.

In today's fast-paced business environment, it's becoming increasingly important to leverage the know-how, testing, and trial-and-error someone else has already done to develop IP including protecting it legally. By collaborating with others and leveraging their IP, you can achieve greater results than you ever could alone.

IP refers to creations of the mind, such as inventions, literary and artistic works and symbols, names, images, and designs used in commerce—brands, for example. IP is protected by law, and owners of it have exclusive rights to use and profit from their creations. One ingenious way of using OPE is to franchise or license one's brand. Sir Richard Branson does this prolifically and very profitably with Virgin. Many of the businesses that appear to be his are in fact mostly owned by others—Virgin Active, Virgin Mobile, Virgin Australia, and Virgin Money, for example. Branson charges fees for lending them the Virgin name, but the actual owners of the business gladly pay it and do all the work because the Virgin brand carries a lot of weight and propels those businesses to a whole other level just because of that IP.

Lots of businesses, such as McDonald's, UPS stores, and

Wendy's, are substantially franchised. They use the OPM of franchisees and charge lucrative royalties for the business format and name. The franchisees are building their empires using those brands' IP. It can go both ways. The franchisor and the franchisee are each OPs to the other.

Leveraging Other People's IP can be more cost-effective than developing your own IP, as it eliminates the need for research and development costs. If developing your own IP is your passion, your lane, by all means, develop away. But if it isn't, then take a look around you and find where someone else has already built what you need. As I mentioned earlier, I have seen a need in the real estate investment space for a robust platform for active and passive investors to use. It should combine tools for all the elements of conscious wealth creation in one place: education, access to opportunities, and mindset. It should be a playground for passive investors and active investors alike. It should combine that education, CRM, legal documents, reporting and compliance, an investor portal, and a way to connect, and it should all be seamless and safe. Nothing this robust currently exists in the marketplace. However, all the pieces do. So I began gathering all those pieces, picking and choosing, and making a wish list. Now that I have that wish list, I will undertake to develop my own amazing software platform for my clients to use. NO, I WON'T! Have you not been paying attention? I found partners, one of whom is a software developer, Jared, who has already built many of the pieces I was seeking and SO MUCH MORE! He and his team will build it with my input because that is not my lane. In fact, it won't even be me who directs the flow of development. My lane is that I came up with the big idea that solves the needs of my clients and our community. We will have a COO who will actually be the one to make sure all the Other People are lined up and get this done because it fits within my stated vision for the company.

Just like in my example of the robust software, leveraging

Other People's IP can provide access to established products and services, which can help to increase revenue and improve the bottom line without literally having to reinvent anything. Not having to develop your own IP can increase the efficiency of your business operations, save you time, and will probably be a better end result because an expert will have been in her own lane while you were in yours.

There are so many ways leveraging OPIP (that's just fun to say) can make your life easier while propelling your business exponentially forward. Improved marketing, for one. Leveraging Other People's IP provides access to established brands and reputations, making your marketing efforts more impactful and likely more profitable. By using Other People's IP with proper licenses and agreements, you ensure you are in compliance with the law and avoid legal issues without having to go through the extensive and expensive process of protecting your own IP, and typically, those OPs will prepare the license agreements, so all you need to do is have your lawyer review and negotiate the terms for you.

Don't underestimate the power of building relationships with the IP holders, which can be beneficial in the long term. When I sought out OPIP for the software platform, I had no idea I would end up finding an amazing partner, and it would spawn a whole new company as a result. The exercise of seeking out my OP was life-changing for all of us.

Leveraging Other People's IP can also help to develop new products and services. Collaboration can lead to new ideas and innovative solutions you might not have thought of on your own. By working with others, you can gain fresh perspectives and insights that can help you take your business to the next level. By collaborating with experts not only in your industry but on the periphery, you can gain access to specialized knowledge and expertise that can help you achieve your goals more effectively without having to invent it all on your own.

The lawyer in me gets especially excited at the idea that when you leverage Other People's IP, you can reduce the risk of making costly mistakes or investing in projects that don't yield results. By working with people who have already achieved success in the area you require help in, you can learn from their experiences and avoid common pitfalls. Remember your lane! You are safer in your lane. And don't give me that BS about nobody making big things happen by playing it safe. There are times to take calculated risks and times to play it safe. The real magic is knowing when to do which. Besides, there's no sense wasting valuable time and resources on research and development when you could be honing your skills and talents or calculating when you should take those big swings. I know it's trite, but sometimes things are trite because they are truisms: Work smarter, not harder. (Forgive me, but I heard somewhere they can't publish business books unless you have at least three such sayings in them. Have you found all three yet in mine? Or more?)

How about a few ways to put OPIP to work for you? Seek out experts in your industry and collaborate with them on projects or initiatives that align with your goals. This could include JVs, partnerships, or consulting arrangements. If you need access to a specific piece of IP, consider licensing it from the owner. Open innovation involves collaborating with external partners, such as customers, suppliers, or academic institutions, to develop new ideas and products. This approach can help you tap into a wide range of expertise and perspectives. If you identify a piece of IP that aligns with your business goals, consider acquiring it from the owner. This could include purchasing patents, trademarks, or copyrighted works. Back when I did mergers and acquisitions for large companies, I often saw the acquiring company make the purchase of the entire company solely for a single patented product. They would shelve all the other valuable IP because the product they wanted was worth the purchase price to their business. I was a young lawyer then, and no one wanted to hear my ideas about how to monetize all that other IP or what a waste it was to acquire an entire company, only to put so much value out to pasture. Alas, I am telling you now. Be creative when seeking out what you need. Someone may just be sitting on it, not even seeing its value. This is where that open communication and telling all your OPs what you need comes in handy.

At the risk of sounding like a broken record, as with anything belonging to someone else, it is essential to obtain the appropriate licenses and permissions and to comply with all relevant laws, including copyright, trademark, and patent laws, whenever you are going to use someone else's protected work. And of course, it's also important to consult with legal advisors before embarking on any IP-leveraging activities, both to protect you and your business from being sued by the owner but also to help you figure out the best way to structure such an arrangement to make the most of it while keeping you the safest.

Other People's Ideas

As I mentioned earlier, using Other People's Ideas is a bit less formal and structured than their actual protected work product. Still, it is legally and ethically important to credit others when appropriate to do so. You see it on social media all the time: photo credits, tagging the author or creator, or indicating you don't know the source but inviting anyone who does to speak up. There is no shame in taking someone's idea and putting your own spin on it. I'd even go so far as to argue that there are no completely new ideas left to be had, only improvements, embellishments, twists, and tweaks to already-existing ideas or new applications of old ideas to different circumstances or facts. I look forward to people messaging me with their completely new ideas no one has ever thought of before. If I get that kind of shade, I will have arrived.

Just like leveraging Other People's anything, OP Ideas can increase the efficiency of your business operations, improve collaboration and teamwork by encouraging open communication and the sharing of knowledge and expertise, build relationships with the idea holders, which can be beneficial in the long term, and help to innovate and develop new products and services. Imagine an environment where idea sharing was not only encouraged but rewarded. I think so many of us get kind of grabby with our ideas and taking credit because we have grown up in a culture of siloed workplaces where backstabbing, idea stealing, and taking unearned credit aided in upward mobility.

Multiple studies over the last several years have highlighted the positive impacts of promoting a collaborative culture that rewards idea sharing in the workplace over fostering siloed competition. One research study back in 2017 by the Institute for Corporate Productivity showed that companies promoting collaborative working were five times as likely to be high performers. However, you have to really mean it. The same study also showed that the main driver was purpose and incentive. This means that you have to not just say you promote sharing ideas; you have to establish a culture that not only supports but rewards it.

Let's use the example of my idea at one of my law firms of advising our large corporate clients how they might monetize their nonessential IP when they acquired other companies. My idea was that if they insisted on buying the entire company rather than only the IP or lines of business they intended to imminently use, they should implement a mechanism to develop, license, or sell the IP and business lines they did not intend to use. Unless the specific purpose was to buy IP to take it out of the marketplace (i.e., shelve it to maintain control of or manipulate a market, which is a rabbit hole I won't go down right now because I do have some thoughts on this tactic), monetizing it was a much better play than to chalk the acquisition cost up to a loss or an inflated cost of the essential IP.

Had the partner I presented the idea to embraced collaborating on an open exchange of ideas to better serve these clients, any number of things might have happened. Sure, one of those things is that the clients could have said something along the lines of "We hired you for the transaction itself, so stay in your lane." (Yes, I recognize that my advice throughout this book has been to stay in your lane, but my lane actually is coming up with creative solutions and strategies for businesses to scale and grow. So even though I didn't have this exact language sorted out in my head yet, I knew this was one of my superpowers. In fact, me actually doing the transactions itself was arguably outside my lane, even if I was good at it.) But the likelihood that the clients would have fired our firm for presenting such ideas was slim. It was pure fear and a scarcity mindset that drove that partner. It drove him to work crazy unreasonable hours for certain clients, it drove him to indulge completely ridiculous client requests (including facilitating some questionable behavior), and it drove him to shut me down when I presented this idea to him.

It's been several years since this happened, and clearly, I am not over it. It seems like such a wasted opportunity, and I don't want that to happen to you. Here's what I believe could have been a more likely, positive, and productive scenario: The partner hears me out because we have created a culture of collaboration and idea sharing that is rewarded. He brainstorms with me to make it even better, talks through pitfalls and possibilities, and learns all he can about what I am proposing. We come up with a pitch together. The partner presents the idea to the client's general counsel as his colleague's initial idea (both appropriate given it was my idea and clever to have cover in case the idea fell flat). The partner proposes an ideation session with the client's general counsel and me to flesh this out even more. We present the idea to the company's executive team; they like parts of it, leave parts of it, add their own spin, and we come up with a plan that works with all the key OP's input and expertise taken into account. I mean, this could make the company millions, or at least save the company millions, and we all could have been lauded as heroes. I'll take my cape in blue, please.

Alas, that is not what happened. And like so many others, not being able to be in my true lane or enjoy a collaborative and supportive environment is one reason I left that firm. Do you have someone like this on your team? Is this you? Embracing OP Ideas can go both ways. You get to leverage those ideas, and in turn you get to support someone else being fully in their unique gifts and talents. Everyone wins, including the client. And when everyone wins, that is how businesses are sustainable and thriving, same as with people.

Whatever the need, it's certain that leveraging Other People's Ideas can provide access to new perspectives and insights, which can help to generate new and innovative solutions to problems. And, as we have seen, creating a culture of sharing ideas creates happier, more productive employees.

"Knowledge, gained through the studying of new information, consists of a rich storage of information. Wisdom, on the other hand, has to do more with insight, understanding and accepting of the fundamental 'nature' of things in life."
–Rens ter Weijde, partner in Purpose+

Other People's Wisdom

As entrepreneurs and business owners, it's no secret that we often feel we have to figure everything out on our own. I hope you are at least now considering that going it alone is not only unnecessary but ill-advised. There is a wealth of knowledge and experience out there that you can tap into, and by doing so, you can greatly increase your chances of success.

One of the main benefits of using Other People's Wisdom is that it allows you to learn from their mistakes and successes. By studying the experiences of other entrepreneurs and business owners, you can gain valuable insights into what works and what doesn't. This will help you to avoid costly mistakes, having your baseline set upon the foundation of OPW. By learning from others who have already been through the challenges you're facing, you can identify potential pitfalls and develop strategies to overcome them. Read books and blogs by successful entrepreneurs and business owners. Subscribe to the YouTube channels of people who are knowledgeable in an area you seek to enter. There are many free and inexpensive resources out there that offer valuable insights into running a successful business, being a happy human, learning how to make money, and anything you want to learn. If your mindset is right, you will leverage all the available education and find there is access to opportunity all around. Make a habit of reading and learning from these sources.

Similarly, a coach or mentor can provide you with personalized guidance and support as you navigate the challenges of running a business. Look for someone who has experience in your industry and who can help you develop the skills and knowledge you need to succeed. A fantastic book on this topic is *The Wise Investor: A Modern Parable About Creating Financial Freedom and Living Your Best Life* by Rich Fettke. This wonderful story about a young man seeking to find his purpose and grow his wealth—who learns more than just basic business principles from his unexpected mentor—illustrates the power of OPW in an easy-to-read story that will probably resonate with any entrepreneur.

But more than just other entrepreneurs' business successes and failures, leveraging Other People's Wisdom can have a much deeper impact on your life and your happiness. Don't underestimate the power of OPW as it relates to your whole being. You presumably want to not only be successful and wealthy but also healthy, happy, and *whole*. I mentioned earlier that one of the best decisions I ever made for myself was to join a mastermind group. A mastermind group is a group of like-minded individuals who meet regularly to share ideas, provide support, and hold each other accountable, maybe not by calling to make sure you did what you said you were going to do, but in the sense you see them regularly, and our nature is to generally not want to let people down. Joining a mastermind group can be a great way to tap into Other People's Wisdom.

One of my masterminds is a forum for the facilitator to share her wisdom and it allows us all to expand our minds so we may create exponential wealth without sacrificing ourselves and our well-being. But we also have one-on-one sessions with her that allow us to really dig deeper into any area we want or need. Sometimes I don't even know what that is going to be until we start talking and she or I have a moment of clarity or insight, and then we keep peeling it back until we get to the root of whatever it is. There is a spiritual aspect to it, not in a religious sense, but in the sense that we are seeking to tap into our own higher wisdom, our connection to whatever source is to us. I like how she describes it because it is almost universal—there is no god language that separates any of us from the others or puts any weight on dogma. There is a time and place for that for some people; this just isn't that place. This isn't an industry-specific mastermind either; it's also universal. Her wisdom helps people see their blind spots and changes their thinking so they can create and exponentially grow conscious wealth.

When I finally started doing the one-on-one work on top of the group sessions, I really began to see everything more clearly. Identifying, defining, and developing my unique gifts and talents was a pivotal moment in my life. Knowing (and accepting) what really lights me up helps me share my gifts with the world, show up as the very best version of myself, make more money, and, while I work a lot, I work only on what I love for the most part. I could not have done that without the benefit of wisdom that was not my own.

What even is your lane? If you don't know, don't be afraid to ask for feedback from others. I don't mean to let others tell you your lane necessarily. Of course, you can ask employees, fellow business owners, your family, or friends what they think your superpower is or how you best serve them. This can give you some interesting insights as to how others perceive you. But when doing this, just be mindful of the fact that many people will respond through their filter of how they perceive you, or more likely, what they need from you. You get to decide what you truly want. But this is a book about leveraging your OPs to get there, and I mean to help you do just that. Your coach, or your mindset strategist, or whichever OP you choose, should be able to help you focus in on your highest self. Looking inward and getting super clear and quiet will draw out your higher purpose. Your lane.

This is where you really need to let go and let your chosen OP shine. To make the most of the wisdom, you have to set aside your ego, limiting beliefs, and your idea of what should be. If you have already achieved your extraordinary life, are doing exactly what you love to do and only that, and have amassed all the wealth you could ever dream of, and your life is as you have pictured it in all your wildest fantasies, then do exactly what you've been doing and don't change a thing. And thanks for reading this far, but I don't think I have anything more to teach you. But if you are like almost every other person in the known universe, then maybe you could stand to have your thoughts shifted just a bit, open your mind, and let some OP Wisdom shine through.

If you are not well acquainted with your higher self, then we need to treat her or him like a really important OP. Through regular self-reflection, meditation, prayer, or whichever language makes you feel comfortable and open to exploring, you can tap into your own higher wisdom from whatever source you believe in, and you can work toward making that higher self an integrated part of you. There are a number of really enjoyable ways to achieve this, and just like with everything else we are discussing, you are not on your own here. Yes, it is *self*-reflection, but that does not necessarily mean always by yourself. I meditate regularly, and I improve and love it each time, but for me, doing the inner work with help and in community with others is like a drug. I want to chase that high and do it more and more.

In-person retreats and events are my favorite way to access both Other People's Wisdom and my own that I am still working toward integrating fully (so for now, my higher self is still somewhat of an OP to me). Yes, of course, attending conferences and networking events is a great way to meet other entrepreneurs and business owners. Take advantage of these events to build relationships and learn from others. However, taking those relationships to a deeper level that allows all parties to really connect and learn to trust one another requires more than just surface-level meet and greets, exchanging of business cards and pleasantries, and then connecting on your favorite social media app. It's a good starting point, but then you need to do the work to take it further. Using Other People's Technology and implementing the help of AI tools can make this more manageable, so long as you take care not to lose the human touch, which is the only thing that can foster true human connection.

Taking those surface-level interactions and entering into masterminds and in-person retreats where you work on not only your business but also your inner self, tapping into all those Other People's inner wisdom and knowledge, is beyond compare. You get to shortcut your mindset, education, and access to opportunities, all while doing things that are fun and feel good. And it's a healthy and beneficial high!

By learning from the experiences of others in a non-judgmental, relaxed, and intimate setting, you can avoid mistakes, expand your network, and increase your chances of success. So, don't be afraid to reach out to others and tap into their wisdom. Or just go to a place where the wise will be and stay near them. Be vulnerable with them. Go inward while they go inward. The collective consciousness is elevated when you do this. You might be surprised at how much you can learn and achieve by doing so. Hopefully, you won't be surprised at all, though. Hopefully, after reading this, you will go with the full expectation that you will grow in ways you never imagined possible. Hopefully, you will go into it so open that you expand your consciousness to create your heart's desire.

The best retreats offer all three elements to create conscious wealth: education, access to opportunities, and mindset. And with the right mindset, you will undoubtedly find that you have the requisite education and abundant access to opportunities all around you. The right mindset often requires some help and support. It requires tapping into wisdom on the regular. It requires knowing what to take in and what to let go.

"In pursuit of knowledge, everyday something is gained.
In pursuit of wisdom, everyday something is dropped."
–Lao Tzu.

My coach helps me in her mastermind and in my one-on-one meetings to do exactly this. It's not like she tells me something I have never heard before. She tells me what I need to hear when I need to hear it. Only then can I actually accept it. And she helps me see what I am holding onto that maybe I need to let go of because it isn't serving me. I am educated. I have read all the books and listened to all the podcasts. OK, maybe not all. But a hell of a lot. Her wisdom in this arena helps guide me to discern which pieces of education, knowledge, and information to employ in the present moment to deal with the present situation. She sometimes tells me which book I need to read next. Sometimes she tells me I need to stop going outside myself for more education and to look inward for clarity. Sometimes she tells me things that make me want to tell her to fuck off. But that's the work.

Is my coach wiser than I am? Well, in some ways, yes. Her wisdom is useful to me because her particular brand of wisdom helps me unlock my own wisdom. She isn't telling me to think like she thinks. She's helping me to think, see, and process in *my* best way, serving my highest purpose. Sometimes, my wisdom is useful to her because sometimes it takes an OP's fresh perspective to see for ourselves what our wisdom needs to teach us. We cannot possibly all have the same life experiences. Find those OPs who have the wisdom from experiences that resonate with you from insights you can feel and a perspective you trust and respect. Then let them shine from their lane!

Other People's Positivity

Earlier, I talked about how devastating it can be to adopt someone's negative mindset. Well, good news. You can access Other People's Positivity and reap the multitude of rewards without putting the pressure on yourself to always be positive yourself—an exercise in futility. Leveraging Other People's Positivity can help you get unstuck when you need a hand there. Let's face it, we all have off days. There are no bad days, if you ask my friend Jeffrey Holst, author of *No Bad Days* (read that one, too), but maybe there are days when we need a little extra love, and we need to borrow that positivity that helps us move through whatever is vexing us. Likewise, lend your positivity to your OPs when they need it, always being mindful of protecting your own energy. Refer back to Other People's Negativity for why you want to avoid energy vampires. All kinds of energy are infectious. Try to surround yourself with as much of the positive, or at least neutral, energy you can. That's not meant to be Pollyanna. I am not advocating for toxic positivity, where we ignore warning signals and negative influences. It means come at them from a healthy place.

My mastermind group used to meet on Monday afternoons. Sometimes Mondays are tough, even when living your extraordinary life, even when thriving in your own lane, or even when your life is mostly bliss. On Mondays, I knew I would be meeting with my people. I knew that I would be bragging. Sometimes it felt like the best brag I could muster was that I actually made it to the mastermind! On Zoom! From my house! But I did show up, because, just like going to the gym, sometimes the hardest part is showing up. Once you get there, your feel-good chemicals kick in, your body and mind know you're doing something good for it, and you leave feeling better than when you arrived. You've heard the phrase "never skip a Monday?" That was my mantra when it came to my mastermind. On the days when I was feeling a little meh, I just let someone else go first. I let them brag about what amazing things they'd accomplished, and I listened to the excitement in their voices. I watched their faces light up with joy and pride. I felt that in my very being. And you know what? I always came up with a brag. I always felt better than when I started. Some days, I would go into the group on fire from a super productive or creative day. On those days, I opted to go first, and I shared that with my OPs so they could watch my face light up, they could hear my voice get excited, and they could feel my positivity.

Doing this in the context of a mastermind or small-group meeting creates a bond with the sharers. Collective consciousness is a powerful tool that we can harness to create massive change in our lives. Leveraging Other People's Positivity helps to build relationships, creating long-term connections. But more important than that, sharing that positivity raises the collective consciousness, which will have a significant positive impact on society by fostering unity, mutual understanding, and shared values. It enables individuals to feel connected to a larger community, reinforcing shared norms and behaviors that facilitate social cohesion and stability. When each of us shares a collective consciousness, we are more likely to work together towards common goals, creating a greater capacity for collective action. Imagine the possibilities in societal advancements if we all approached interactions with people in this way. Our meetings would serve as a catalyst for social change, magnifying awareness of societal issues and motivating collective efforts to address them. In essence, the shared beliefs and moral attitudes functioning as a unifying force promote cooperation, empathy, and the advancement of societal well-being. While you are feeling good and building your empire, if you're doing it using Other People's Positivity and lending yours, you can also be impacting something bigger, something global. Now, *that's* power.

Leveraging Other People's Positivity can provide a learning opportunity, combining the education and mindset elements of conscious wealth creation in one powerful exercise. Not only can you learn from their experiences, thoughts, and perspectives, and use that knowledge to improve your own mindset, you will also create new neuropathways in your brain as you do this, allowing you to call on this learning more easily in the future.

Allowing Other People's Positivity to help you train your own brain will have a significant and lasting impact on your own life and well-being. When you see others achieving their goals and tackling challenges with a positive mindset, it inspires you to do the same by providing you with evidence that it can be done. Positive people tend to be motivated and driven, and their energy can be infectious. Seeing this evidence of success and positivity makes it easier to see the good in things and maintain a positive outlook on life. When you're in a positive environment, you feel happier and more optimistic, which builds upon itself the same way negativity and pessimism do. Remember, whatever you feed your constant, you get back exponentially. Feed it positivity, even if you have to borrow it from others as you develop that muscle or if you have a setback. It gets easier and easier to overcome challenges, and you become more resilient the more you teach your brain how.

Did you know that positive people tend to have better mental health than those who are negative or pessimistic? Surrounding yourself with positive people can help you to manage stress and anxiety and may even reduce symptoms of depression. This is not an invitation to ignore your mental health in favor of hanging around positive people, but rather a suggestion that hanging around such people is going to be better for your overall mental health than hanging around negative people. Not rocket science, but science nonetheless.

Want to enhance your social connections? Positive people tend to attract other positive people, and being part of a supportive and uplifting social network can help you to build strong relationships and feel more connected to others. Someone who is either naturally positive, and even more so when someone has put in the work to become positive, is going to take care to not let negative people bring down their energy. If you want to be around powerful, impactful people—and I would wager you do—then you need to learn from them and then become a positive force for when they need you to be their OP as well.

Other People's Thinking

Bad attitude? Steal someone else's until you get your shit together. As an empath, I protect myself by stopping energy vampires from bringing my energy down, and being around positive people is a good step. However, taking that even further, you need to surround yourself with people who have a way of thinking that works to achieve your extraordinary life. Beyond positivity, all the way to the belief systems you need to adopt to really live your heart's desire. I am talking ridiculous, audacious, out-of-this-world belief in your ability to have literally everything you truly want. This is likely going to come from more than one other person, and just like when you partner with or enter into a trust relationship with anyone else, I would encourage you to really do your diligence here. Not every smooth-talking guru who wants to sell you a dream life truly has the thinking you want to adopt. (In fact, I would advise you that the best gurus don't want you to adopt their way of thinking; rather, the good ones want to help you develop your own way of thinking that is best for your own higher purpose.) So, how is it they claim to know what you should be doing? What is the feeling you get from them? You know when someone comes across as off? Trust that. What is their experience? Who else that you know, like, and trust also knows, likes, and trusts them?

Leveraging Other People's Thinking provides access to new insights and entirely new belief systems. Please understand, I am not telling you to simply abandon all your deeply held beliefs in favor of someone else who appears to have what you want. I am, however, telling you to closely examine all your beliefs to determine which of those is working for you now and which of those it may be time to let go of. Most of our beliefs were formed way before we were consciously choosing them—before the age of five. Those beliefs were either passed down from others around us (many of which we definitely do *not* want to adopt) or maybe developed as a way to survive whatever our situation was at that time.

I have an overdeveloped sense of responsibility. That most definitely did not come from the adults around me when I was young, but it was developed as a way to survive a childhood where the people around me were barely able to take care of themselves, let alone a small child. My parents were teenagers and still in party mode when I was little. I have distinct memories of taking care of other small children at an age when adult me would not even have left my daughter home alone. I was tasked with cleaning the house and taking care of my siblings while my parents were gone. This massive sense of responsibility served me well. I was praised by adults, and I saw it as a way to get love. I also thought I needed to be responsible for everyone around me being safe. As one does, I carried that well into adulthood.

It has taken years of coaching and near-constant reminding that I am not responsible for everyone around me. I have surrounded myself with Other People who set healthy boundaries and who respect mine. Their thinking has shown me that I can be responsible for myself and not be considered selfish or (shudder) irresponsible. Occasionally, I will fall back into being responsible Bethany. She is not the best Bethany. She is overstressed. She over-thinks. She does not take very good care of herself. That oxygen mask everyone tells you to put on yourself before helping others? She will gasp for air while emptying the plane. And if that were healthy, and she was happy while doing it, then she would look like a hero. But she is no hero. She used to *think* she was. That is, until her healthy, right-thinking Other People gently showed her that she is really the best for her Other People when she is well cared for and thriving.

A bloodletting martyr is not who I ever wanted to be! Ick. Leveraging Other People's Thinking about what it means to be responsible and what it does not mean helped me improve my decision-making about how I spend my energy and how I show up for others and for myself. It even helped with my efficiency in my business operations, as I no longer do things that are not mine to do simply because I feel responsible for everything. What's even better is that this way of thinking has fostered collaboration and teamwork. When I am not in a vacuum doing everything, I am open to not only accepting help but also to better ways to get things accomplished.

My favorite part about this is that once I opened my mind to various ways of thinking, I was able to proactively choose which ways worked for me. It was a conscious choice and not simply allowing things to happen to me. I finally had full responsibility for myself. Once you have that, once you see evidence of how it works in your favor, your brain keeps finding the evidence to support it. The awesome result of that is that it gets easier and easier to snap back out of old habits, even if you slip from time to time. And slip, you will. But that's OK. You can look to your OPs, or you can even just remind yourself of their thinking to get yourself back on track.

Chapter 8
OPK
Other People's Knowledge

In the business world, knowledge is power. As a business owner or entrepreneur, it's important to understand that you don't have to know everything. There are experts and professionals who can provide you with the knowledge and insights you need to succeed.

One of the primary benefits of leveraging Other People's Knowledge is that it allows you to access expertise you don't have yourself, are not equipped to, or are not interested in acquiring. Leveraging Other People's Knowledge allows you to make better decisions and avoid costly mistakes. Another benefit of leveraging OPK is that it allows you to stay up-to-date with the latest industry trends and best practices without the time and expense of learning it yourself. The business world is constantly evolving, and it can be challenging to keep up with all the changes. By tapping into the expertise of others, you can stay ahead of the curve and position your business for success.

So, how can you leverage Other People's Knowledge to your advantage? For starters, refer to Other People's Networks (see Chapter 9). Build a network of experts and professionals in your industry who can provide you with valuable insights and advice. Attend industry events, join professional organizations, and connect with people on social media to expand your network. Pay attention to what Other People's lanes are so you can call upon them when the need arises. Consider hiring advisors or consultants who have expertise in areas where you need help. For example, you could hire a financial advisor to help you manage your finances or a marketing consultant to help you develop a marketing strategy. Attend training and development programs to improve your own skills and knowledge. This could include workshops, seminars, or online courses. You need to keep your own expertise sharp so that your Other People will feel comfortable being in your sphere. Conduct market research to gain insights into your industry and your customers. This could involve conducting surveys, focus groups, or analyzing industry reports. You must know which lanes need to be filled and what level of expertise you need to seek out.

To really double down on Other People's Knowledge, look for opportunities to collaborate with other businesses that have complementary knowledge and expertise. For example, you could partner with a company that has expertise in a particular area to develop a new product or service. Both businesses can leverage the other to scale more quickly and efficiently.

I'm at a point in my life where I have acquired most of the knowledge I am going to. My brain feels full, and I now need to apply that knowledge toward achieving my dream life. If I learn even one more fact, I feel like I will have to forget someone's birthday or how to put on pants. No one wants that. Obviously, I am joking. Sort of. I will be a lifelong learner, and I can just keep the stuff that's relevant to me top of mind and maybe forget some of those pesky negative things we discussed at the beginning of the book. But with age and wisdom, I am getting significantly better at seeking out people with the knowledge I need and letting them apply it to what I need to have done. There are a lot of things I could learn but just can't want to. "Can't want to" became my favorite explanation for why I would not be doing something when Mackenzie was a toddler—it was the line she declared to me whenever refusing to do something requested of her. "I can't want to, Mama." That is really the most honest answer, isn't it?

I've learned through a ton of self-reflection that even though I have historically had the GSD (Get Shit Done) attitude most entrepreneurs have, getting shit done is not actually my highest and best use. I am a big ideas person. I know how to come up with business models that will solve problems and make money. I can listen to what people need, and I can create a solution to help them. But when I am bogged down with the tasks required to implement the visions I create, then I am less creative, more stressed, and actually less productive. I don't always know how to implement my big ideas. I know the strategy, the desired outcome, and maybe even some roadblocks to look out for, but I don't always know the best way to get there. Once I realized that, or rather admitted that, I allowed myself to seek the knowledge of Other People and take those tasks off my plate. Those Other People, rather than seeing me as lesser than for not having all the required knowledge, actually thanked me for getting out of *their* way and allowing them to GSD in a way they knew how. They didn't want to come up with the big ideas or be responsible for them. They wanted to GSD. Bless them! I got the hell out of their way, and we all took off.

I used to say, "The people saying it can't be done should get out of the way of those of us doing it." (I still say that, so who am I kidding?) But what I realize is that sometimes those people with the big ideas get in the way of the people actually getting shit done by jumping into the wrong lane. I was one of those people.

Once I stopped, my businesses began to grow and thrive, and one woman I hired to help me with marketing and social media even referred to me as a thought leader in my industry. What? (Thanks, Jade.) I finally allowed others to shine in their respective crafts, and *then* I was able to really be in my genius zone (credit to psychologist and author Gay Hendricks for this brilliant term). All of this was possible because I asked for help and leveraged Other People's Knowledge.

So, the moral of the story is this: Don't be afraid to reach out to others and ask for help when you're trying to achieve your wildest dreams. By leveraging Other People's Knowledge, you can learn faster, make better decisions, and achieve your goals more quickly and efficiently than you ever could on your own.

Other People's Content

In the digital age, where content is king and the online landscape is a bustling metropolis of ideas and creativity, the concept of leveraging Other People's Everything (OPE) takes on a new dimension. Specifically, the power of leveraging Other People's Content can become a strategic asset in expanding your influence and growing your brand.

Using Other People's Content can be a highly effective strategy for achieving success, whether you're running a podcast, social media account, or any other type of online platform. But in order to do it right, you need to understand the principles behind content curation and how to use it to your advantage.

In the digital landscape, where every scroll brings a new story and every click unveils a world of knowledge, the savvy content curator thrives by mastering the art of leveraging Other People's Content. Imagine embarking on this quest for content curation, where the pursuit is not merely for content but for connections, credibility, and community. Picture yourself as a curator in this vast digital gallery. Your mission is to select only the most exquisite pieces—content that resonates with the very heart of your brand and echoes the interests of your audience. You navigate through the endless streams of articles, videos, and social media posts, seeking out those that are crafted with care, rich in information, and bursting with engagement.

As you gather these treasures, you understand the importance of honor and tribute. Giving proper credit to the original creators is not merely a courtesy but a cornerstone of your ethos. It's an act that forges respect, trust, and perhaps, paves the way for collaborations that weave your narratives together in the future.

With each piece of OPC you share, you imbue it with your essence. A dash of commentary here, a sprinkle of insight there—it's your unique perspective that infuses the shared content with new life. This transformation not only distinguishes your brand but elevates you to the realm of thought leaders, a voice among the echoes that stands clear and true. Your gallery grows, each addition curated with purpose and regularity. You stay attuned to the ever-changing rhythms of your industry and have a consistent presence in the dynamic conversation of your field.

And the rewards? They are multitudinous (thanks, Word a Day Calendar). Your digital domain becomes a hub of engagement, a place where your audience gathers not just to consume but to converse and connect. Your brand, once a solitary voice, now sings with the chorus of the community you've built. And let's not forget the hours saved and resources conserved—precious time that you can now invest in other pursuits, thanks to the rich content others have crafted.

Your website, a beacon in the online expanse, grows stronger in its foundations as the SEO (search engine optimization) benefits of shared quality content begin to take hold. The backlinks and traffic are the byproducts of your strategic curation, the organic growth beneath the soil of your digital presence. Yet, amidst this curation of shared content, the brushstrokes of your originality remain vital. OPC is not a replacement for your own creation but rather a complement—a balance of give and take, a harmony of originality and curation. Much like this chapter.

In leveraging OPC with intention and thought, the reach of your success extends far beyond the horizons you once knew. It is a dance of mutual growth, a shared path toward a destination richer than you could ever forge alone.

And now that you've learned this important lesson, unless you are a social media expert, you really should simply be sharing content that resonates with you with your OP, the one who manages your social media content. Once you find someone who understands your voice, your brand, and your style, give them the same direction we discussed in the chapter on delegation. And then let go! I have recently hired not one but two social media experts to help me with my influence and brand in anticipation of the release of this book. One of them is charged with the overall strategy and voice, making sure that everything we post is true to who I am. The other is to blow up my engagement and reach exponentially with proven marketing techniques. Both are experts in their respective areas, have worked with people whose brands I have followed for a long time, and are dedicated to helping me reach my goals by staying in their lanes and letting me stay in mine.

One of the strategies employed is to provide video hooks for me to use for my content. I give the prompts my own spin to make them authentic for me. Sometimes, I choose not to use a prompt that doesn't resonate with my personality, even with tweaks. My social media manager and her team make sure that whatever I use from the prompts does not dilute my brand or rip off anyone else's brand in any way. It's a team effort, but the point is that I just show up and deliver what I am good at, and they do the rest. Lanes.

Other People's Teams

Life, in many ways, is like an intricate symphony. Each instrument plays a vital role, but it is the harmony of them all together that creates something truly extraordinary. Similarly, in the quest for a magical life, one's unique gifts and talents are the solo performances that stand out, yet they shine brightest when complemented by the strengths of others—particularly the coordinated efforts of a team.

Leveraging Other People's Teams means engaging the collective expertise of individuals who have honed their skills in areas different from your own. This is not just about delegation; it is about collaboration. It's about recognizing that you can't—and shouldn't—do everything yourself if you want to truly excel.

When you focus on what you do best and delegate the rest, you have more time to innovate and improve your own skills. You effectively maximize your own talent. A team can work on multiple facets of a project simultaneously, greatly accelerating progress. Teams bring diverse perspectives that can spark creativity and lead to more innovative solutions. Spreading the workload prevents burnout, allowing you to maintain energy and enthusiasm for your work. Working with Other People's Teams allows you to enjoy all these benefits without having to lead and manage those particular players, leaving you completely free to play where you most want to be.

As I have mentioned throughout this book, the first step is introspection. What are your unique gifts and talents? These are the activities you are not only good at but also enjoy—those that put you into a state of flow. It cannot be overstated that once identified, the goal is to spend most of your time in these areas. If you have skipped this step up until now, stop what you are doing, take a moment to really reflect on this, and come back once you have defined your lane. Call your Other People and talk it through if you need help. There is no shortcut on this one. This prerequisite will make all the other things you do meaningful.

Now, with your strengths in mind, seek out Other People's Teams whose skills complement your own. These teams may come from professional networks (think consultants or freelancers who bring specialized skills), business partnerships where the businesses have a vested interest in your mission, virtual assistants, or local or online communities that offer support and services.

Effective team collaboration requires clarity, communication, and mutual respect. Make sure you define what you aim to achieve with the help of the team. Establish transparent channels for feedback and updates. Trust your chosen team with their tasks and avoid micromanagement. Acknowledge the team's contributions to encourage motivation and loyalty.

The relationship with the team you leverage should be symbiotic. As they help you grow, look for ways to contribute to their development. Share knowledge, provide growth opportunities, and be an advocate for their services.

Working with Other People's Teams comes with challenges such as differing work cultures, communication styles, and expectations. Address these challenges by setting clear agreements, using collaborative tools, and being open to learning from each experience.

Your Action Plan

(I told you I wasn't going to let you skip this part!):

1. **List Your Strengths:** Write down what you're great at and love to do.
2. **Identify the Gaps:** Note what tasks you are currently doing that take you out of your flow state.

3. **Research Potential Teams:** Look for those who excel in the areas where you need support.
4. **Engage and Clarify:** Reach out and establish clear objectives and expectations.
5. **Evaluate and Adjust:** Regularly review the arrangement to ensure it's working for both parties.

By leveraging Other People's Teams, you not only optimize your own talents but also contribute to a larger ecosystem of success. Remember, building a magical life isn't a solo venture—it's a collective pursuit. Surround yourself with a team that not only supports your mission but also shares your vision, and together, you will create a masterpiece.

If you don't get good at delegating, your business will suffer, and your goals will remain out of reach. Delegation is an essential skill for any business owner. It allows you to leverage the strengths of your team and focus on the areas of your business where you can add the most value. Dan Martell, author of *Buy Back Your Time,* says, "Delegate what you do that *others* can too until you only do what *only you* can do." That's a mouthful. What he means is that you should reserve your time and energy for things to which you are uniquely suited. Don't waste your time doing things others can do for you. He also says something I freaking love, which is "80 percent done by someone else is 100 percent freaking awesome." Leverage your OPs.

But beware! There is such a thing as bad delegation. This occurs when you delegate tasks to the wrong people or fail to provide clear instructions and guidance. If the leader (psst, that's you) is not clear in her vision, communication of that vision, and her expectations for the outcome, then she sets her team and her goals up for failure. This can lead to a range of problems, like poor quality work, confusion and frustration among your team, burnout and resentment, and damage to your reputation and credibility.

Never fear—I wouldn't dare give you a problem without a solution (something else you should implement with delegating, by the way). When you take a proactive and intentional approach to delegation, you will be more effective. The most important thing to remember has been a recurring theme throughout the book: Once you have determined which tasks are squarely in your lane, you can identify the right tasks to delegate to your OPs. You're looking for tasks that are time-consuming or require skills that your Other People possess. Of course, when delegating tasks, choose OPs who have the necessary skills and experience to complete the task successfully. They should know their lane just as you know yours. Provide clear guidance, including deadlines, expectations, and any relevant details. Beware this one! This does not mean micromanage. It means to be clear about the outcome you expect and give over any information you have that is pertinent to your definition of success. Giving guidance does not mean telling your OPs *how* to deliver whatever it is you've requested. When you choose the right *who,* they will handle the *how.* That said, clearly communicate your expectations for the quality and completion of the task. The person to whom you have delegated should have a clear picture of what success looks like to you. Create an atmosphere where asking for clarification is welcome and offer support and guidance as needed. Finally, feedback on completed tasks should be provided, the strengths of the OP should be recognized, and constructive criticism should be offered for areas of improvement. Done effectively, this will free up so much of your time and mental bandwidth and will allow you to focus on the things that only you can do to create your extraordinary life.

Chapter 9
OPN
Other People's Networks

I t may be trite and cheesy, but it's true that your network is your net worth. And Other People's Networks can be just as valuable to you. Maybe even more so. One of the superstar OPs in my network is Ed Mathews. Ed, a real estate developer, speaker, mentor, and host of the *Real Estate Underground Podcast*, says, "Building relationships is the only way to succeed in the real estate investing game, with investors, brokers, and building owners." With permission, here's Ed's framework for building a valuable network:

1. **Build awareness.** Provide content to create a perspective in the marketplace, whether that's a blog, podcast, social media, speaking, or whatever. Give away your missile secrets. Do it willingly and without expectation.
2. **Make friends.** People like working with people they like. But here's the hitch... become *actual* friends. Hang out. Get to know them. Help them out. Be there for

them in good times and bad. Continue serving them without expectation.

3. **Build trust.** Over time, you will earn their trust, and they will earn yours. Be worthy of that trust. Continue to serve them without expectation.

4. **Earn the right to do business.** After some time, you will earn the right to do business together, but not a moment before.

It's straightforward, but it's certainly not easy. Building a real estate investment business, just like building any other business, is not a get-rich-quick proposition. Get over it. It takes time, character, empathy, integrity, and a commitment to serve. You're building a foundation made of hardened concrete and steel. Leveraging Other People's Networks allows you to widen that foundation exponentially.

Once you have built this foundation, it can sustain an enormous empire. I mean, OPs are one thing. OP's OPs? Now *that* is literally exponential. Let me tell you the story of how I leveraged my own trusted network and their networks to buy a freaking hotel!

It started with my dream to travel the world hosting retreats to help people scale their businesses and create and grow conscious wealth in the beautiful properties I co-owned. I envisioned it with my mindset strategist, and we came up with some goals and plans. I started reaching out to my OPs to fill in the gaps that fell outside my now well-defined lane.

One of my first calls was to David Kafka, a client and friend. I knew David had raised OPM for resort properties already. I knew he was a real estate agent in beautiful Belize, and he's a client of my securities law firm, Premier Law Group, so I trusted that he was serious about doing things the right way. At first, I just asked David to be on the lookout for properties suitable to host retreats

—to rent out to start, but eventually to acquire something. He responded right away with, "Actually, I've got an off-market deal with a fantastic seller who doesn't really want to sell, but he's had a once-in-a-lifetime opportunity come up and he needs to move back to the U.S. It's a killer deal and he will work with buyers he likes and trusts to take care of his staff."

I was intrigued, to say the least! I immediately started researching the property—an 11-room boutique beachfront hotel in Placencia, Belize. I read the valuation, Trip Advisor reviews, and I booked a trip to visit the property and meet the seller and staff. At that point, it went from intrigue to straight-up love!

The hotel was already profitable. The seller had bought it just after the world began to open up after COVID-19. He'd invested some money into it, rebranded it, improved it, built an all-star staff of hardworking and trustworthy rock stars to run the day-to-day, and he loved it like his baby.

I have to say that the seller being such a stand-up guy helped me feel confident about this deal. David knew him well, the staff just loved him, and even the local airport staff, upon learning I was going to the Mariposa, said, "Mr. Lewis' place? Tell him we say hello! He's such a good guy." They even took a selfie with me to send to Lewis! Lewis is well respected in the community, supports the local economy, and treats the staff like family.

OK, but I know better than to buy real estate on emotion alone. Run the numbers, and the numbers will tell you what to do. I knew what Lewis was asking, and it seemed more than reasonable, but I had to know for sure. This was decidedly *not* my lane, so I sought out another OP to help me with the pro forma and financial diligence. We did this even before we put in an offer. Since it was an off-market deal and the seller wasn't in too much of a hurry, there was less pressure to rush into anything. It was perfect for my first foray into the active investor lane.

At the time, the hotel had six treehouses and five beachfront rooms. There were already plans drawn up for six new treehouses, and I liked that plan, so we ran the numbers for that, keeping it conservative and not increasing other revenue over the prior year for existing rooms or for food and beverage. But given my master plan was to host high-end retreats and our real estate community is a bunch of event hosts and attendees, we added revenue for six retreats during off-peak season to see where we landed. The financial whiz who helped me, who came out of public accounting and whose default answer is "no" to investments, told me, with this plan, "This thing cash flows like a motherfucker!" (My new favorite metric for analyzing deals, by the way.)

So, the numbers were good. But we were acquiring not only property but foreign entities owning the property and operating businesses (the hotel and the bar and restaurant). Good news here: This is at least partly in my lane. Having done mergers and acquisitions for a big chunk of my legal career, I know a thing or two about legal diligence and acquiring operating businesses. I just needed someone in Belize to check the local law and a real estate transactions lawyer to help. I went back to my OPs, who had my back.

We went ahead and put in an offer to see if we could move it forward. The offer was accepted! David and I had about a million conversations with the seller, so we all knew what everyone needed from the deal, and we had already done the work to make sure it made sense.

So, with a purchase price of $3.8M, $1.6M of that being carried in a note by the seller (remember in Chapter 4 we talked about this creative use of OPM), plus the projected cost to make the improvements I wanted, plus some reserves for working capital, I needed to raise about $3M. To do that responsibly, though, I needed to make sure I had partners who could help me make this vision a reality: someone who could help oversee the construction of the treehouses, someone who could help market and host incredible events alongside me, and partners who shared my vision and ideals to help implement the processes and technology and improve efficiency and profitability while I led the vision to scale this into a world-class destination for anyone seeking to create conscious wealth while nourishing their soul.

David, being an expert on Belize and luxury properties there and also being physically near the property, was a natural fit, and he was eager for the opportunity to partner on a property he's already been enjoying for years as a guest and friend of the seller.

I'll admit the next one was harder for me. I thought I needed a hotel operator who had also specifically raised OPM for a boutique hotel out of the country. I was a little stuck here. That is a really small needle in a really big haystack. I did research. I talked to other active real estate investors. I talked to my mindset strategist to see if I was missing something or needed a perspective shift. I meditated on it and looked inward to see what I really needed.

Here's what I came up with: The hotel was being run well by local staff and an owner who was only there part-time and also had never run a hotel before (who also agreed to stay on and advise me for five years!) I know what it takes to scale businesses, I know my lane and I know how to use my OPs to fill open lanes, and I know what I want to see for events and for marketing the hotel. What I really needed was someone to help me market, promote, and host epic events and help me take this property to the next level. It was already a gem, but it could be a diamond once everyone saw what we'd done with it.

Enter my friend, Britt Arnason, DIYer turned influencer turned real estate investor. She had all the things I needed for this project, *and* she had already told me about her vision for her career, and this was perfectly aligned. I made the call, she did her diligence, and she said yes. So we brought along a crew to document it all, and we met David in Belize to get this thing going! We busted our asses, but it was such a fun ride at the same time.

Something else Britt had that helped in making her an excellent marketer was a vast network that she had organically cultivated over the last several years. She allowed me to access that network to make this dream a reality, and it helped us both get what we wanted. Her followers wanted to know all about what we were creating, and it expanded my ability to share my gifts and talents with a whole new world of amazing people. When Britt told her network about our hotel, another guy reached out to discuss what he wanted to create, which led to another and so on. Exponential.

When you want something, all the Universe conspires to help you achieve it.

To book a room at the
Mariposa Belize Beach Resort

SCAN THE QR CODE
and use the discount code

BETHANYFRIENDS20

Discount Code: BETHANYFRIENDS20

Other People's Relationships

My daughter Mackenzie, who is 17 at the time of publishing, is interested in possibly becoming a make-up artist for models, actors, musicians—any kind of artist. She is really good at it, she loves it, and she wants to get paid to travel the world with cool and interesting people. She also loves music and film, but she does not want to be in the spotlight. It is a well-thought-out dream, actually. Yet, she has already been met with, and has to some extent begun to internalize, that this is not a safe or steady occupation but more of a hobby and that it would be too unpredictable to count on it to make a real living. While she doesn't necessarily need a college degree for this particular career path, she is applying to go to college to make sure she has a backup plan and an education to fall back on and also to learn business practices to turn this into something she can rely upon. My practical mother side wants to celebrate her responsible attitude and her cautious realism. But my inner goddess is screaming out to her to go all in with her dreams and find her OP to make it a reality. Go to college, sure, but not just to have a backup plan or something to fall back on. Go to college to learn which OPs she will need and to meet them! Go to college because it is good to accomplish something that is difficult and takes a long time because that builds character. Go to college because she is fortunate enough to have parents who will pay for it so she does not graduate with crippling debt before she even gets started. Go to college because it is fun, and you need to learn to live on your own. Even go to college in case you change your mind and you want to explore and create options for yourself. But for the love of all that is good and pure, do not go to college because you don't fully believe in your dream or in your ability to live a magical life. You will be doomed to live a life that is not the extraordinary life you deserve and have everything within you to create if that is your mindset.

Notice I did not say you will be doomed to fail. You will fail—lots of times. You must fail. Some of our best learning is in failing. However, do not mistake the good kind of failing with continuing to do things best suited for others with less than desirable results. The lesson to be learned is that you need to find your OP and let them use their unique gifts and talents to help you build your empire.

Using my daughter as an example, what Other People would she need to find to make sure she could pursue her dream and do what she loves and excels at? She could find the artists and the models to show them how talented she is so they can use their influence and relationships to make sure she is the one on set with them. But how does she get in front of them? Does she build up her social media to attract the attention of the artists? NO! That is also not her talent, nor is that something she loves to do. She does not want to be in the spotlight, she does not want to be a social media influencer, and she does not want to cold call artists. She would need to find someone who knows how to get her in front of the right people to showcase her talents. I love my daughter and I believe in her, and many of us tell our kids they can do or be anything they want. And that is true, to an extent. That is not the hard part. Knowing *exactly* what they want and doing *only* that is the real trick. That takes a lot of self-reflection and self-awareness.

This is the trap so many of us fall into. We don't stay in our lanes. I am guilty of it as well, and it is a constant exercise I am doing. We need to keep at it every single day. Like anything that makes us better, we have to be consistent and do the reps. To have a healthy body, we need to eat well and move our bodies consistently. The same is true of our mindset and mindfulness. The same is true of our learning. The reason I continue to build my network and consume educational content and meet with my advisors and attend my mastermind is that I am exercising a muscle. That does not end. You are never done. And that may seem daunting, but it is really very liberating and freeing. You will always have help. You will always have reminders of how to build your empire more easily, efficiently, and effectively. My mastermind group reminds me that I should not be doing my own social media or scheduling my own meetings, or handling the details of my retreats. If I am not being reminded, I tend to fall back into old habits (the conditioned self) of just trying to do everything myself. Continuing to do that will leave you exhausted and frustrated and will not get you the extraordinary life I hope you are envisioning for yourself.

Let's break it down: What does leveraging Other People's Relationships get you? The obvious one is access to new connections, which can help to expand your reach and find new opportunities. Every single time you are at an event or in any room, figure out who you don't know but need to know. Remember what my friend Ashley Wilson said: You should lead with what you have to offer, not what you need. You are someone that some of those people need to know as well. Show up for them. You also get instant increased credibility when someone else vouches for you. A testimonial is way better than you touting how awesome you are. Your marketing will improve as your brand becomes associated with the right OPs. (Notice I said the *right* OPs. Remember how I told you to vet those? Do it.) Along those lines, leveraging Other People's Relationships can help to increase your visibility, as it can provide access to new audiences and potential customers. Expanded reach is immensely valuable. Referrals from OP's Relationships are going to save you time and money relative to developing each new relationship from scratch. Leveraging OP's Relationships can help you gain access to knowledge, information, and resources that can benefit your own business that you might not even have thought of. Just be sure to engage and actually develop these relationships and take care of them. A poorly treated referral or lack of follow-through will surely damage your relationship with the person whose original relationship it is and word travels fast. Protect your reputation by protecting theirs when they allow you into their networks.

Other People's Social Capital

This is a little different from Other People's Content and Other People's Networks, but in the same vein. This is where mentoring,

OP's Networks, Relationships, and Experience all roll into one big benefit to you.

Imagine walking into a room—a huge networking event, let's say—where you know nobody. Now imagine walking into the same room arm-in-arm with the event's respected host. Suddenly, every introduction is warmer, every handshake firmer, and every smile brighter. Why? Because someone of influence, someone trusted, has endorsed you. This is the essence of leveraging Other People's Social Capital.

But what exactly is social capital? At its core, social capital is the collective value of all social networks and the inclinations that arise from these networks to do things for each other. It is an intangible asset, a type of wealth that can be invested in and spent, but not in the way you might spend financial capital.

A while back, I was invited to speak at a client's event. I hadn't met many of the people in attendance, and I didn't know most of the other speakers. Even though I know my subject matter well (in this particular case, the securities rules relating to real estate investments), I felt like a phony compared to the big names speaking before and after me. I walked through the sea of people, feeling like I did not belong and was not adding as much value as the famous keynotes. Then, my client took the stage to introduce me personally as his company's SEC lawyer. Instant credibility. My imposter syndrome began to fade away just as I was about to take the stage. Eyes were fixed on me, and people listened to my every word. Not because I was as engaging as the keynote or because I had some polished professional talk (although I do like to think I've come a long way in that regard over the past several years), but because the guy they all came to see, the guy who put on the event, told them he trusted me enough to not only hire me as his company's lawyer but to invite me to take the stage at his biggest event of the year.

Fast forward to a couple of years later, and I was speaking at another client's event. This time, I walked through the event knowing I was adding value to the attendees, but there were a few speakers I didn't know, and once again, I felt inferior somehow because they were influencers or famous. Then my client started a group chat with all the speakers. I was in a group chat with these people I thought were so above me. Don't get me wrong; I am confident in who I am and what I do, but I am also a human who sometimes forgets herself. One of the other influencers chimed in, "Bethany, my SEC lawyer, I LOVE her!" It was like he gave me permission to be on equal footing with those Other People I didn't know just from that endorsement. Maybe I didn't need it. Maybe they assumed I was someone, or maybe they didn't even think about it at all. But in my mind, that influencer lending his social capital allowed me to make the most of that event and develop meaningful relationships with people I might not otherwise have had the confidence to connect with.

When you leverage Other People's Social Capital, you are borrowing their trust, their connections, and their influence to advance your purpose. It's like having a key to doors that would otherwise be closed to you. But this isn't about manipulation; it's about forming genuine relationships where both parties benefit. How does this work? Well, first off, you get the advantage of accelerated access. That is, by connecting with influential individuals, you gain access to resources, information, and opportunities at a much faster rate than you could on your own. Then there's the enhanced credibility. When someone with established credibility vouches for you, their endorsement provides you with instant credibility. This is crucial when you are just starting out. You get near-instant expanded reach. Other People's Social Capital can extend your reach into communities and networks that would otherwise take years to penetrate.

Ever wonder how people gain thought leader status, giving them increased influence? It's in part by having the backing of influential individuals who can amplify your voice and your ideas. By surrounding yourself with Other People who have achieved what you aspire to, you gain insights and knowledge that can fast-track your growth.

It is important to approach this with the mindset of mutual benefit—it must be a two-way street. The principle of reciprocity is powerful. You must also be willing to contribute to the pool of social capital. This could mean offering your own expertise, sharing valuable information, or connecting people within your network with each other. Some of my favorite Other People are those who speak well of me even when I'm not in the room. Do the same for your favorite Other People, and it will go a long way to paying attention to this social capital concept.

To start building and leveraging Other People's Social Capital, first look for Other People whose interests and values align with your life's purpose. Authentic engagement fosters trust. Be genuinely interested in what your Others are doing and find ways to support their initiatives. Before asking for anything, find ways to provide value. People rushing to meet their own goals can neglect the part where you need to share your knowledge, offer your help, or connect your Other People to resources.

This is another one of those ongoing maintenance situations. Keep in touch with your network. Social capital doesn't thrive on one-off interactions but rather on sustained relationships. When you connect members of your network with each other, you become a hub of connections, thereby enhancing your own value within the network. My good friend, Nate Robins, is a pro at this. Every time we talk, he asks me, "How can I support you?" And it's genuine. He is willing to go out of his way to support me and my community, and I trust he knows I will do the same for him and his community. That's how it works. And isn't that how we should all be with each other? I think so.

When you leverage Other People's Social Capital effectively, it creates a ripple effect. Each person you connect with, each relationship you deepen, and each piece of knowledge you acquire and share adds to the pool of collective wealth. Your purpose becomes interlinked with the purposes of others, creating a synergy that can propel you forward in ways you never imagined. Think of your life's purpose as a blueprint. Leveraging Other People's Social Capital allows you to fill in that blueprint with rich experiences, relationships, and knowledge. It helps you construct a life that is not just about personal achievement but also about community and connection. And isn't that the very fabric of a dream life?

Social capital is all around you, waiting to be engaged. The question is, how will you tap into this vibrant resource to build your extraordinary life? How will you ensure that the borrowed influence becomes a bridge to not only your success but also to the enrichment of those whose capital you share? Your extraordinary life is not just a destination; it's a collaborative experience.

Other People's Families

You do not owe anyone access to you. That is a privilege that must constantly be earned. It is OK to love someone from a distance. This one might be a little controversial, but hear me out. I believe in personal choice *and* personal responsibility. Sometimes we are born into situations that are not ideal for the kind of success or conscious wealth we want to create, but we cannot take on the negative mindset or limiting beliefs of Other People, even if those people are our original family. It is perfectly acceptable to love your family and not have them in your inner circle if doing so is at the expense of your peace, health, happiness, or ability to achieve whatever level of success you have decided is right for you. Understanding this and accepting this allows you the freedom to make the choice about how you conjure your extraordinary life. You are not saddled with the responsibility to hang onto relationships that don't serve your highest and best good. You are not obliged to sacrifice yourself to maintain something you were born into. Fully embracing this also forces you to take personal responsibility for your own success because you can no longer point to your original family, your upbringing, or your born-into circumstances as the reason you have not achieved what you want to achieve.

As adults, we have the option to choose who we spend our time with. We can choose Other People's Families! I have close friends who are like family to me. We spend holidays and birthdays together. My two best friends, Alex and Richie, are a married couple, and their kids are like my kids, and my kid is like theirs. Their extended family has become like family to Mackenzie and me. My sister Danielle has become like family to them. Their whole family refers to her as Aunt Dani. Other People's Families can provide that closeness, and the best part is, like with any other important factor of your magical life, you choose it.

Other People's Children

My former law partner, Mauricio, offered this gem to me mostly in jest. But there's something to it. This younger generation is making more conscious decisions about having kids. Rather than simply having kids because that is the expected next step in life, the younger generations are establishing careers and enjoying freedom. And some people simply cannot have children of their own. That said, Other People's Children can be an awesome way to get your fix of those interesting and funny tiny humans without the lifelong commitment to growing them into productive adults. I mean, I love my kid, but this is genius.

In the realm of entrepreneurship, where the ticking of the clock is as valuable as the chime of currency, the decision to start a family is one of profound consequence. For those teetering on the edge of this life-altering choice, there exists an intriguing alternative: the joy and resourcefulness of engaging with Other People's Children. The untold benefits of what might be considered borrowed parenthood offer a perspective that cherishes freedom while embracing the vibrant energy of youth.

For the entrepreneur, life is a canvas of calculated risks and strategic moves. Introducing children into this mix is not a decision made lightly. So the lesser-walked path of Other People's kids can offer the laughter and lightness of children without the full-time commitment. This chapter isn't about shying away from responsibility but the strategic and joyful engagement in young lives, which enriches your own.

Consider the first, and perhaps most talked-about aspect of young parenthood: diaper duty. It's a rite of passage for many, yet by sharing moments with Other People's Children, you sidestep this task and instead focus on the more joyful aspects of interaction. There's a special delight in handing back the child at the first scent of foulness, allowing you to return to your entrepreneurial endeavors with renewed energy.

Then, there's the pure, unbridled entertainment that children provide. Their imaginations are boundless universes where the mundane becomes magical. By joining in their creative play, not only do you tap into this fountain of joy, but you also invite a freshness of perspective back into your own life and work. The laughter of a child can be the best medicine for an overworked mind. Moreover, the time spent with these young minds is fertile ground for unexpected learning. The way children see the world, their curiosity, and their capacity for simple joy can teach you more than you'd expect. Whether it's the architecture of an impressive pillow fort or the strategy behind a new board game, these skills can translate into creative problem-solving and innovation in your business pursuits.

Networking, too, takes on a different hue in the company of

children. Today's playdate is tomorrow's potential business meeting. The families you meet and the parents you converse with during a child's birthday party are connections that can blossom into future collaborations. And who's to say that the child whose imagination you once fueled won't become a mover and shaker in their own right, with you fondly remembered as an influencer in their early years? Your niece or nephew or bestie's spawn may just be the icebreaker you need to strike up a conversation with the CEO of that new tech company. Don't get it twisted; I am not saying use your friends' or family members' kids for your own gain, like in some hokey sitcom where the guy takes a kid to pick up women. I am simply saying that being in the presence of Other People's Children can have some benefits you might not have considered. Just keep it cool. It never worked out for the weirdo who used a kid to pick up.

The financial and temporal savings of not having your own kids are non-negligible as well. In this economy, where every dollar and hour counts, engaging with rather than raising a child can mean more resources devoted to your entrepreneurial ventures. The cost of childcare and the time commitment of parenting are substantial, and while they are undoubtedly worthy investments, they are not compulsory for everyone.

Finally, the liberating truth: When you're spending time with Other People's Children, the weight of responsibility is lightened. You have the unique opportunity to influence and inspire, to teach and cherish, without the round-the-clock accountability that parenting entails. It's the freedom to invest in young lives but also to step back and recharge, ensuring that you can give the best of yourself both to the children you borrow time from and the business that bears your name.

Starting a family is a deeply personal choice, each with its own set of rewards. However, for those who seek a different path, the experiences borrowed from engaging with Other People's Children offer unique benefits—freedom, joy, learning, and connection, all without the enduring responsibilities of parenthood. It's a path that leads to personal and professional growth, enriched by the laughter and wonder of the youngest among us. So, the next time the parental urge nudges at you, remember the world is full of children whose lives you can touch without changing diapers.

Chapter 10
OPE+
Other People's Energy

Have you ever noticed how some people seem to effortlessly exude positive energy while others seem to drag you down with their negative vibes? As a business owner or professional, it's important to recognize the power of using Other People's Energy to help you achieve your goals and create success in your life. The truth is that energy is contagious. When you surround yourself with positive, high-energy people, you'll find yourself feeling more motivated, inspired, and creative. On the other hand, when you spend time with negative, low-energy people, you may find yourself feeling drained, discouraged, and unmotivated. This chapter is about tapping into the collective vigor, enthusiasm, and dynamism of those around us to build a wealth that's mindful and impactful.

Imagine wealth as a garden. In it, your ideas are the seeds; your capital and resources, the soil and water. But to make those seeds sprout and your garden flourish, you need the sunlight—energy. It's the vitality from mentors, partners, employees, and even customers that breathes life into the soil, transforming seeds into saplings and saplings into a lush canopy. It's the OPs that make the magic stuff happen.

Energy is an intangible asset that propels businesses forward. It's found in the passionate work of a dedicated team, the enthusiastic feedback of loyal customers, and the inspiring guidance of mentors. By harnessing this energy, entrepreneurs can propel themselves toward creating conscious wealth—wealth that does good, feels good, and continues to grow.

In the world of business, the energy we speak of manifests in various forms. A motivated team can push innovation, overcome challenges, and drive the business forward. As a leader, channeling this energy towards your vision can lead to breakthroughs and achievements. Enthusiastic customers don't just bring repeat business; they bring new customers. Their energy, in the form of support, advocacy, and word-of-mouth, can be more effective than any marketing campaign. The sage advice of experienced mentors carries an energy that can light the way through tough decisions and uncertain times. Collaborative partnerships combine the energies of different entities, creating a powerful force that can open new markets and opportunities.

Create an environment where energy can thrive. This means values-driven leadership, open communication, and recognition of efforts. Truly engage with your customers, team, and partners. Listen to their ideas and feedback, and use this energy to refine and improve your business. Delegate with trust. Empowering others to take ownership of their work unleashes their energy in ways that micromanagement never will. When looking for employees, partners, or mentors, seek those whose energy aligns with your mission and values. Alignment amplifies energy.

Harnessing Other People's Energy requires a conscious approach. It involves being a leader who not only directs but also listens, learns, and adapts. It's about being an entrepreneur who understands that the energy of those around you is not a resource to be exploited but a powerful current to be shared, a force that grows as it's given.

As we forge paths toward wealth, we must remember that our OPs power all that we set out to achieve and experience. By leveraging OP's Energy, we tap into a wellspring of potential that can elevate our ventures to new heights. It's not just about the energy we use, but also about the energy we inspire. This is the essence of building conscious wealth—wealth that's sustainable, regenerative, and a testament to the collective power of human spirit and endeavor.

"Building conscious wealth" is not a tagline for social media likes or branding; it's a mission statement, a vision that honors the role of human energy in crafting businesses that are not only successful but also sustainable, ethical, and empowering. Our community, the Conscious Capital Collective, was created specifically to harness this type of communal energy.

So, how can you tap into the power of Other People's Energy to achieve your goals? Surround yourself with positive, high-energy people. Seek out friends, colleagues, and mentors who are positive, supportive, and inspiring. Spend time with people who lift you up and help you see the best in yourself and your business. Pay attention to the energy of the people around you, and learn from their examples. Watch how successful entrepreneurs and business leaders handle challenges and setbacks, and take inspiration from their resilience and determination.

While it's important to surround yourself with high-energy people, it's also important to set clear boundaries and protect your own energy. Avoid spending time with people who constantly complain, criticize, or bring negativity into your life. Collaboration is a powerful way to tap into the energy of others and achieve your goals. Look for opportunities to collaborate with other business owners, professionals, or organizations to create mutually beneficial partnerships. One of the best ways to tap into the power of

Other People's Energy is to give back to your community or to causes you care about. When you give of your time, talent, or resources, you'll not only make a positive impact on the world, but you'll also attract positive, high-energy people into your life. An important guidepost in selecting any OP, but particularly Other People's Energy, is that you should only surround yourself with—and take advice or direction or energy from—Other People living a life you admire and would like to emulate for your own life.

Lean on your OPs when you are feeling low energy, and be ready to step up and step in when you need to be that OP for someone else. The power of using Other People's Energy is a key ingredient in creating success and achieving your goals. By surrounding yourself with positive, high-energy people, learning from the energy of others, setting clear boundaries, collaborating, and giving back, you'll tap into the power of Other People's Energy and create a positive, successful, and fulfilling life and business.

Other People's Mistakes

It's a truth universally acknowledged by entrepreneurs and business professionals that the path to success is littered with the debris of past errors and failures. While there's undeniable value in the hard-earned lessons from our own blunders, the mistakes of others offer a wealth of wisdom, often at a much lower cost. There's an invaluable art to turning hindsight into foresight, learning from the missteps of others to steer clear of potential pitfalls in our own ventures.

To harness the lessons from Other People's Mistakes, a mindset of unending curiosity and learning will serve us well. As with everything in life, we must keep our eyes wide open, our minds ready to absorb, and our egos in check. Every misstep made by another is a beacon warning us of dangers beneath the surface, helping us navigate clearer waters ahead.

Most successful people are all too willing to share their mistakes to help those of us on the way up. I mean, who doesn't love a redemption story? It's OK to want to stare at all the train wrecks you see in business, so long as you take the lesson from them. Carnage for the sake of carnage is just sadistic.

And if you're really paying attention, patterns emerge. Like a detective at a crime scene, we can identify the usual suspects—be it inadequate financial foresight, a disconnect with the customer base, or flawed operational executions. Recognizing these recurring themes allows us to be proactive in protecting our own enterprises against similar fates. And let's face it, it's much easier to spot the patterns and mistakes of others, whether they are sharing or we are simply observing, because we aren't so close to the situation. I'm quite certain I have been the subject of a cautionary tale or two. Maybe even just today. We learn and we grow and we keep going.

But the learning doesn't stop at recognition. You've got to put what you learn into action or it doesn't mean shit. It could mean revamping our financial controls, honing in on customer satisfaction metrics, or even overhauling our business model if that's what it takes to pivot away from potential disaster.

As we benefit from the misadventures of others, we should also contribute to this collective pool of knowledge. By openly sharing our own faux pas and what they've taught us, we enrich the community, creating a culture of transparency and growth. Whenever I share the mistakes I have made with clients seeking my counsel on how to scale, it seems to do two important things: 1) It drives the point home in a clear and concrete, real-life way, and 2) It makes me more relatable because I am a real human who has overcome real things, and I've achieved some level of success as a result of the lessons I've learned.

The study of Other People's Mistakes is less about reveling in schadenfreude and more about recognizing the generosity in these lessons. As business owners, we're afforded the opportunity to build upon the ruins of past dreams, to avoid the traps that ensnared others, and to aspire to heights we might otherwise have only imagined.

Other People's Experience

In the quest for wealth and success, one of the most invaluable resources that often remains untapped is Other People's Experience. There exists transformative power in leveraging the wisdom, insights, and lessons learned from others to build not just wealth, but conscious wealth—wealth that is mindful, ethical, and sustainable.

Other People's Experience is a reservoir of knowledge gained through years of triumphs and setbacks. It's a collective wisdom that, when tapped into, can guide you through the labyrinth of business and investment decisions, helping you avoid pitfalls and capitalize on opportunities.

The benefits of tapping into Other People's Experiences are multifaceted. It accelerates your learning curve, allowing you to bypass common mistakes and embrace effective strategies. The insights from seasoned professionals provide a much-needed reality check, aiding in a more accurate evaluation of risks. It fuels innovation, encouraging creative solutions to old and new challenges. Moreover, connecting with experienced individuals often leads to broader networking opportunities, unlocking doors to potential partnerships and collaborations. Most importantly, learning from others aids in making informed ethical decisions, ensuring your path to wealth aligns with a broader impact on society and the environment.

To effectively leverage Other People's Experience, you can go about it in a bunch of different ways. Seeking mentorship or coaching from those who have a proven track record in your field of interest is one of my favorites. Attending industry events and conferences helps connect with and learn from experts. Collaborative projects offer an opportunity to work alongside experienced professionals, absorbing their knowledge firsthand. Diving into books, case studies, and historical data provides diverse perspectives and experiences. Lastly, practicing active listening and observation in interactions with successful individuals can offer profound insights into effective decision-making processes.

When I first undertook to build the Conscious Capital Collective, the community I had envisioned would blossom from the robust technology platform I mentioned earlier, I had all these ideas and all these plans and, quite frankly, I was overwhelmed at the sheer possibility of it all. It was when I finally started asking my OPs about the communities they've built and the platforms they've used that it all began to take shape. To the surprise of exactly no one, I was overthinking it, making it more difficult than it needed to be. My OPs had experience that was relevant to what I wanted to create. One client told me to actually offer *less* than I originally intended, saying it might confuse or overwhelm people trying to navigate and put to practical use the tools I wanted to provide. Another person told me which technology did and did not work for him and his community. Using all this collective insight, we built a community that is significantly better, and will provide much more value than whatever I would have built had I done so in a silo, referencing only my own thoughts, ideas, and experiences.

Reflecting on real-life examples, like an entrepreneur who attributes her success in a particular industry to the lessons learned from a former industry leader or someone whose partnership with a veteran investor opened doors to profitable and conscious real estate ventures, underscores the tangible impact of Other People's Experience. However, it is crucial to approach this with a mindset of critical analysis. While learning from others, it's important to analyze the advice and adapt it to your unique context. Avoid over-reliance on a single source of experience, or else you may find yourself with a narrow viewpoint that isn't even your own. Seek diverse perspectives to ensure a well-rounded understanding of whatever it is you are building. As with everything, pick the parts that work for you and your extraordinary life and leave the rest.

Strategically absorb wisdom to make smarter, more conscious decisions in your wealth-building endeavors. Learn from the past to forge a future that is not just financially prosperous but is also ethically sound and sustainable.

Other People's Systems

Michael E. Gerber, in *The E Myth Attorney*, astutely cautioned attorneys about the need to shift from running a law practice to running a business, emphasizing the importance of harnessing the power of Other People and a well-defined system. But what about the magic that happens when you combine the two? What happens when you seek solutions beyond the confines of your own industry and start exploring Other People's Systems? This is where true innovation and exponential growth can occur.

In your journey toward building your empire, whether it's in the realm of law or any other field, there is immense value in studying and adopting systems that have proven successful elsewhere. The adage "Don't reinvent the wheel" has never been more relevant. While there may be few law firms that perfectly align with my vision for my legal business, there are countless other types of businesses with systems I can borrow, adapt, and integrate to propel my empire forward. And that's exactly what my team and I have done.

When we were looking to streamline our client intake process and enhance our client experience, instead of painstakingly developing a new system from scratch, we looked outside our industry. For example, top-tier hospitality brands meticulously cater to their guests, creating a seamless and memorable experience from the moment they step through the door. We can borrow elements of their check-in procedures, customer service training, or personalized interactions to transform our law firm's client onboarding process. We have read myriad business books and have taken bits from each of them. Same as I've done to write this one.

The beauty of exploring Other People's Systems lies in the opportunity for cross-pollination of ideas. When you step outside the confines of your own industry, you're exposed to diverse approaches, innovations, and best practices. These fresh perspectives can ignite your creativity and inspire you to reimagine your own systems and processes. Let's say you run a technology startup, and you're looking to streamline your product development cycle. Instead of solely consulting technology industry experts, venture into the realms of manufacturing, where lean and efficient processes reign supreme. Can you adapt principles from just-in-time manufacturing to optimize your software development pipeline? The possibilities are endless when you embrace the wealth of systems available beyond your immediate field of expertise.

The key to leveraging Other People's Systems effectively is adaptability. While it's tempting to transplant a successful system from one industry to another, it's often necessary to tailor and fine-tune it to align with your unique goals and values. For example, a healthcare executive seeking to improve patient care through efficient scheduling might draw inspiration from the airline industry's approach to optimizing flight schedules. However, she must carefully adapt and integrate these principles into the healthcare environment, accounting for the unique needs and dynamics of patient care. We found this especially true in our highly regulated law business, where our client base is also in the highly regulated business of selling securities. Adapt effectively and you win.

In the grand scheme of empire building, OPE takes on a new dimension when you incorporate Other People's Systems into your arsenal. In this approach, I am not suggesting mere imitation but creative synthesis—a harmonious blend of ideas and methodologies that transcend industry boundaries.

As you navigate the path toward conscious wealth, dare to explore the wealth of systems beyond your immediate domain. Open your mind to the possibility that the perfect solution to your challenges might exist outside the walls of your industry. Embrace the diversity of thought, the cross-pollination of ideas, and the adaptability required to make these systems your own. In doing so, you'll not only accelerate your success but also carve a unique and remarkable path toward building your empire—one that is driven by the wisdom and innovation of Other People's Systems, all woven into the fabric of your own visionary empire.

Other People's Causes

Giving to Other People's Causes is a powerful and transformative act that will create a positive impact on the world and enrich the lives of both the giver and the receiver. Contributing to causes beyond our immediate sphere has a profound influence on our Other People.

When you contribute to Other People's Causes, you initiate a ripple effect of positivity that extends far beyond your initial act of generosity. Your support will inspire others to join the cause, amplifying the impact exponentially. It's a chain reaction of goodwill and compassion igniting meaningful change in communities, societies, and the world at large.

When we tap into the deep well of compassion within us, it reminds us of our shared humanity and the interconnectedness of our lives. As you extend a helping hand to those in need, you experience a profound sense of fulfillment and purpose. It is a reminder that your actions have the power to alleviate suffering, bring hope, and make the world a better place.

Contributing to causes outside your immediate circle broadens your perspective. It exposes you to issues, challenges, and realities that you may not have encountered otherwise. This expanded awareness fosters empathy and a deeper understanding of the diverse range of struggles and aspirations that exist in the world. It can also lead to personal growth and a heightened sense of gratitude for your own blessings.

Through building a legacy of impact that extends beyond your own lifetime, your contributions will benefit generations to come. Whether it's supporting education, healthcare, environmental conservation, or social justice, your actions can leave a meaningful imprint on the world.

The concept of Other People's Everything (OPE) is intricately connected to giving to Other People's Causes. Just as you can leverage the resources, skills, and knowledge of others to advance your own goals, you can also leverage your own resources to support causes that align with your values and aspirations. By doing so, you become a catalyst for positive change while strengthening your connections with like-minded individuals who share your passion for making a difference.

There are numerous ways to give to Other People's Causes, ranging from financial contributions to volunteering your time and expertise. You can support local charities, international organizations, grassroots initiatives, or causes close to your heart. The powerful result is a force that transcends boundaries and transforms lives. It is a testament to our shared humanity and the potential for positive change that resides within each of us. As you embrace the principles of OPE and extend your support to causes that resonate with you, you not only make a difference in the world but also enrich your own life in profound ways.

Remember that giving is not limited to financial contributions; it encompasses the act of sharing your time, skills, and resources to uplift others. You don't have to be a billionaire to lend support. Whether you choose to support causes on a local or global scale, your contributions, no matter how big or small, have the power to create a brighter, more compassionate world for all. And what better team-building experience than improving the lives of others while learning about the people around you? One goal of my business is to select a cause near and dear to the hearts of our employees each month and support that cause as a company. Everyone gets to participate and learn what is important to everyone else on the team. I just love a scenario when everyone wins, don't you?

Chapter 11
OPMS
Other People's Mindsets

We've already explored how leveraging the resources, connections, and skills of others can propel you forward, but now, finally, we dive deeper into the treasure trove that is Other People's Mindsets. Mindset is the mental blueprint that shapes our beliefs, drives our decisions, and ultimately determines our destiny. It's a force so powerful that it can single-handedly create or destroy fortunes. When you embrace the power of OPE, you unlock limitless perspectives, attitudes, and paradigms, all of which can drive you toward conscious wealth and empire building.

Remember Coach Nate, my swim coach who guided my first-ever meditation, arguably one of the most impactful of my life? He had a mindset that believed if we relaxed our bodies and cleared our minds the night before a race, we would show up better for ourselves and our team. I realize that meditation is fairly commonplace and openly discussed now, but this was back in 1991, and I had never even heard the word before. In fact, I don't think he used that word at all, and we just did a listening exercise on the pool deck. His mindset may also have been that perhaps no one would embrace his "wild" or "woo woo" tactics in 1991 Ohio; I don't know. What I do know is that after getting a glimpse of his vastly different mindset, I had a truly life-affirming experience that is still impactful all these years later. Borrowing his mindset expanded my own in ways I am still discovering.

I am in love with the concept of a mindset multiverse. The idea is akin to the boundless expanse of our universe, teeming with galaxies, stars, and planets. However, instead of celestial bodies, it pertains to the infinite diversity of human thought, beliefs, and perspectives.

Imagine, for a moment, that each individual's mind is like a unique galaxy in this mental universe. Just as galaxies have their own distinct characteristics and configurations, a myriad of factors shape each person's mind, such as their upbringing, experiences, culture, education, and personal beliefs. As a result, the mindset multiverse is filled with countless ways of viewing the world, solving problems, and approaching life's challenges.

In this mental cosmos, there are limitless possibilities for innovation, creativity, and problem-solving. Just as the universe contains an infinite number of stars and planets, the mindset multiverse harbors an endless array of mental landscapes, each offering its own set of possibilities and insights waiting to be explored.

Moreover, much like celestial bodies interact through gravitational forces, individuals within the mindset multiverse can collaborate and engage with one another. When people with different mindsets come together, we have the potential to combine our unique perspectives to tackle complex problems and drive innovation. It's akin to the gravitational pull of galaxies, drawing us closer and creating new constellations. This mental cosmos is not static; it is dynamic, constantly evolving, much like our expanding universe. We can learn, grow, and reshape our mindsets over time. By seeking out diverse experiences, engaging in lifelong learning, and being open to new ideas, we can continually expand our mental horizons, just as the universe continues to expand.

In this vast expanse of thoughts and beliefs, we have the power to shape our own mental universe. By consciously choosing our beliefs, attitudes, and thought patterns, we can create a mindset that aligns with our goals, values, and aspirations. We can also draw inspiration from Other People's Mindsets to help refine and expand our own, like a skilled astronomer observing distant stars to better understand their own cosmic neighborhood.

Understanding the concept of the mindset multiverse is a powerful tool for personal and professional growth. It means recognizing there are a myriad of ways to approach challenges and that different perspectives can offer valuable insights. It encourages individuals to become more open-minded, adaptable, and effective in their endeavors, just as astronomers use powerful telescopes to explore the depths of space.

In essence, the concept of the mindset multiverse underscores the richness and diversity of human thought and perspective. It is a reminder that, much like the universe itself, our minds are filled with boundless potential and uncharted territories waiting to be explored. Understanding and appreciating this concept can empower individuals to navigate the complexities of life more effectively and contribute to the collective evolution of human consciousness, much like intrepid explorers charting new territories in the universe.

One of the most compelling aspects of OPE, then, is the diversity of mindset it offers. Every one of us possesses a unique perspective shaped by our life experiences, cultural background, and personal beliefs. When you open yourself up to the collective wisdom of others, you gain access to an infinite array of thought patterns and approaches to problem-solving.

Consider the entrepreneurs, innovators, and visionaries who

have shaped our world. They didn't achieve greatness in isolation; they drew upon the insights and perspectives of countless others. Henry Ford's assembly line revolutionized manufacturing, but the efficiency principles of Frederick Taylor influenced it. The work of calligraphy expert Robert Palladino inspired Steve Jobs, the iconic co-founder of Apple, to create beautiful fonts for his computers.

By embracing OPE, you can tap into a rich tapestry of ideas and philosophies that can reshape your own mindset. Whether it's seeking out mentors, engaging in meaningful conversations, or consuming the wisdom of great thinkers through books and courses, the possibilities are limitless.

Belief is a cornerstone of conscious wealth creation and empire building. Your mindset shapes your beliefs, and your beliefs shape your reality. When you surround yourself with individuals who possess a wealth-consciousness mindset, their belief systems can infuse your own with the confidence and conviction necessary for success. Imagine being in the presence of someone who has already achieved the level of wealth and empire you aspire to build. Their unwavering belief in the possibility of your success can be infectious. It can help you overcome self-doubt, navigate challenges, and stay committed to your goals. Additionally, when you leverage the mindset of others, you gain access to a wealth of information and strategies that have worked for them. You can learn from their mistakes and successes, adapting their proven principles to your own journey.

Collaboration and Innovation

The power of OPE extends beyond personal growth and belief. It's a catalyst for collaboration and innovation. When you combine your own unique perspective with the mindset of others, you create a fertile ground for groundbreaking ideas and solutions. Think of the most successful companies in the world today. They thrive not only because of their individual brilliance but because they harness the collective intelligence and creativity of their teams—their Others. By fostering a culture of diverse thought and leveraging OPE, they continually push the boundaries of what's possible.

In your quest for conscious wealth and empire building, seek out partnerships and collaborations with others who possess complementary mindsets. Embrace the diversity of thought and perspectives within your team, for it is in this melting pot of ideas that innovation truly flourishes. And always remember that you are not alone. You have at your disposal a vast universe of OPE to draw upon. Embrace this power, cultivate it, and use it to reshape your beliefs, drive your actions, and fuel your success.

The wealth of perspectives and experiences available through OPE is a gift waiting to be unwrapped. By leveraging your Others, you'll not only accelerate your progress but also open the door to a world of possibilities you may have never imagined. So, surround yourself with those who inspire, challenge, and uplift you, and together you'll chart a path to conscious wealth and empire building that is truly remarkable.

Other People's Everything

I've shared with you a bunch of concepts, each crucial to my journey towards success and to the success of those I've encountered on this path of leveraging OPE. Now, it's time to roll up our sleeves and dig into the practical application of these concepts in your quest for a magical life.

When I was a kid, I loved the show *Silver Spoons*. It might have been the beginnings of my lifelong crush on Jason Bateman. Anyway, in that show, as the name suggests, the main character's dad is super rich. The icon of that wealth to me, as a kid, wasn't the house or the car or the household help. I mean, I noticed all those things, and I knew one day I'd also love to have them, but what absolutely blew my mind was that they had an arcade-sized video game. In. Their. House. It stuck with me all these years. So when I moved into this gorgeous home that I love, I wanted Mackenzie to experience what I imagined Ricky Schroeder's character to have experienced, being able to play video games without quarters at his home. It's not nearly as exciting to her as it is to me, but it's one of those things I always wanted as a kid, and my inner child got it for my adult self.

For me, then, the first step was to adopt the mindset of possibility. Before seeing the show, I didn't even know it was possible for people to have video game consoles in their homes. And then I saw it. I saw an example of what was possible. And from that example, I let myself dream and believe. This belief opens doors and shatters limitations. Start by recognizing that there are countless opportunities and resources available to you through OPE. Cultivate a sense of curiosity and wonder, always searching for ways to leverage the talents, skills, and knowledge of others to enhance your own journey. And let go of that silly notion that putting your OPs to work for you is lazy or leaves you undeserving of incredible success. On the contrary, building your OPE network is essential to it. Identify the people, organizations, and communities that can contribute to your success. This could include mentors, advisors, peers, or even online communities. Reach out, establish connections, and foster relationships that are mutually beneficial. Of course, OPE is a two-way street, so be prepared to offer your skills and expertise in return.

As discussed earlier, systems play a pivotal role in achieving success. Examine your current processes and operations and consider how you can implement or improve systems to streamline your efforts. Explore Other People's Systems from diverse industries, adapt them to your needs, and continuously refine them for efficiency and effectiveness.

A growth mindset is the cornerstone of continuous improvement. Embrace challenges as opportunities for growth, and don't let setbacks deter you. Learn from your experiences and from the experiences of those in your OPE network. Be open to new ideas and perspectives, and be willing to adapt and evolve.

Collaboration is the fuel that ignites innovation. Encourage collaboration within your OPE network, combining your strengths with the strengths of Others to tackle complex problems and generate creative solutions. Keep the lines of communication open and create an environment where ideas can flourish.

To make the most of OPE, you must have clear goals and a strategic plan. Define your vision for a magical life and break it down into actionable steps. Use the resources and expertise within your OPE network (and those provided in the Conscious Capital Collective) to support your journey. Most importantly, taking consistent action is key to achieving your goals.

Understand that OPE is a reciprocal concept. Just as you receive support and resources from Others, be ready to give back. Share your knowledge, experiences, and resources with those who can benefit from them. Paying it forward not only strengthens your network but also creates a positive ripple effect in the broader community.

Masterminds and Retreats: My Favorite Way to Build a Better Business *and* a Better Life

In the quest for success, building a better business is only one part of the equation. Equally important is crafting a better life that aligns with your vision and values. It's more than just achieving financial prosperity; it's achieving a sense of fulfillment and purpose. Hands down, my favorite way to simultaneously build a better business and a better life: masterminds and retreats.

Masterminds are gatherings of like-minded individuals who

come together to share knowledge, experiences, and ideas. These gatherings harness the power of collective intelligence, allowing participants to tap into a wealth of diverse perspectives and expertise. The result is a synergy that can propel both your business and personal growth to new heights. One of the most compelling aspects of masterminds is the opportunity to surround yourself with success—the power of proximity. When you engage with individuals who have achieved what you aspire to, you gain direct access to their wisdom, strategies, and insights. Their experiences become your roadmap, helping you navigate challenges and make informed decisions.

Masterminds create an environment of accountability and goal setting, sure. But the best ones go beyond that and are actually transformational. When you share your goals and aspirations with a group of motivated peers, you're more likely to stay committed and take meaningful action. The collective support and encouragement provide the fuel you need to turn your dreams into reality.

In addition to business benefits, masterminds foster meaningful relationships. The connections you form can extend beyond professional collaborations, leading to lifelong friendships and a supportive network that transcends business dealings. These relationships can enrich your personal life and provide a sense of belonging.

Retreats take the concept of masterminds a step further. They offer an immersive experience that combines learning, relaxation, and self-discovery. Retreats often take place in inspiring locations, providing an ideal backdrop for reflection and growth. Retreats encourage you to step away from the hustle and bustle of daily life and dedicate time to personal growth. Whether it's through workshops, meditation, or outdoor activities, retreats allow you to reconnect with your inner self and gain clarity on your life's purpose and values.

One of the essential components of building a better life is achieving a healthy work-life balance. Retreats offer the opportunity to unwind, recharge, and recalibrate. They remind you that life is not just about business success, but also about personal well-being and happiness.

What sets masterminds and retreats apart is their practicality. The insights and skills you acquire during these experiences can be directly applied to your business. You learn not only how to excel professionally but also how to lead a more fulfilling life.

Masterminds and retreats are my personal favorite way to build a better business *and* a better life because they embody the principles of Other People's Everything at their core. By surrounding yourself with motivated and like-minded individuals, you leverage the collective intelligence and experiences of Others to accelerate your growth. Moreover, these gatherings emphasize the holistic nature of success. They recognize that true prosperity is not confined to financial achievements alone but extends to personal fulfillment and well-being. In a world where the lines between work and life can blur, masterminds and retreats provide a structured yet enriching approach to building a life that truly reflects your values and aspirations.

Embrace the power of masterminds and retreats on your journey toward conscious wealth, empire building, and a more magical life. As you immerse yourself in these transformative experiences, you'll not only see your business thrive but also witness the profound impact on your personal growth, happiness, and overall fulfillment.

Especially in this digital age, it's easy to rely on technology to connect with others and conduct business. And that can be super effective. However, there's still something to be said for the power of face-to-face interactions. In today's fast-paced world, we tend to get caught up in the day-to-day demands of running a business. But taking time to step back and reflect on your goals and vision is essential for long-term success. The best way to do this is by attending an in-person retreat.

In-person retreats provide an opportunity for team members to collaborate and brainstorm ideas in a new and refreshing environment, leading to increased creativity and innovation, as well as new perspectives and ideas. They provide an opportunity for team members to work together in a face-to-face setting, which can help to improve collaboration and teamwork, and lead to more effective problem-solving and decision-making.

Offering a chance for team members to connect and communicate in a more relaxed and informal setting improves relationships and creates stronger communication skills, which will benefit the team long after the retreat has ended. Your team members will enjoy the opportunity to communicate in real-time, helping to resolve issues more quickly and improving decision-making. By stepping away from their daily routines and focusing solely on the retreat activities, individuals will invariably increase their productivity and focus, fostering a renewed sense of purpose and motivation. Team members working together to solve problems in a face-to-face setting is proven to be more effective than communicating remotely. Fun and data-backed? Count me in.

Disconnecting from work and other stressors with a specific focus on personal well-being will reduce stress levels and improve mental health, benefitting individuals and the team as a whole. And any opportunity for team members to bond and build relationships outside of the office will enhance your company's team culture, providing you have taken the important step of defining and communicating the desired culture, which you can also accomplish at a retreat.

Stepping away from the distractions of everyday life and focusing on your goals and vision for your business, while feeling like a vacation of sorts, will actually lead to greater clarity and direction in your work. This change of scenery refreshes the mind and inspires new ideas.

All these benefits to your *self* and your business can usually be written off as a business expense. Lawyer disclaimer time: I am not a CPA or tax advisor, so check with yours about how to report these awesome adventures on your taxes.

Meditation with your OPs, at a retreat or otherwise, has some really intense benefits for all involved. For one, when people meditate together, they share a collective experience of calm, peace, and mindfulness, creating a sense of unity and interconnectedness, reinforcing the idea that we are all part of a larger whole. Many forms of meditation encourage practitioners to cultivate feelings of loving kindness and compassion towards themselves and others. When practiced collectively, empathy and understanding among group members cannot help but seep through.

There's a concept that the collective energy of a group can be greater than the sum of its parts. In the context of meditation, this means that meditating as a group can amplify the positive effects of the practice, forging a stronger sense of peace and well-being than individuals might achieve meditating alone. You want stronger bonds between yourself and your OPs? Meditate with them. It creates a space for people to connect on a deeper level, beyond the usual surface interactions.

Sharpening Your Axe: The Importance of Preparation

In the realm of conscious wealth creation and empire building, Abraham Lincoln's timeless wisdom, "Give me six hours to chop down a tree and I'll spend the first four sharpening my axe," reverberates with profound significance. These words encapsulate the essence of preparation—the indispensable cornerstone of success.

The value of preparation cannot be overstated. It serves as a guiding light, illuminating the path to success with clarity and purpose. Why is it so crucial? Preparation empowers you to discern your priorities and craft a well-defined plan of action. Armed with this roadmap, you can maintain laser-like focus, ensuring that your efforts are channeled toward the most critical tasks and objectives. As we all know, time is an irreplaceable resource, and preparation is the key to making the most of it. When you prepare in advance, you can sidestep costly mistakes and minimize wasted time. Your understanding of what needs to be done and how to do it becomes a guiding light, making quick work of your otherwise complex challenges. Proper preparation equips you to deliver higher quality work and achieve superior results. This not only enhances your reputation but also attracts new customers and clients, laying the foundation for long-term success.

Whenever I have to give a talk or presentation, I get nervous only when I have not thoroughly prepared. Crowded room? No problem. Tough topic? Piece of cake. Disorganized or unprepared? I lose confidence. And confidence is that critical ingredient required to get you through challenges and setbacks. Knowing that you've prepared diligently instills a deep sense of self-assurance. Armed with this confidence, you can approach challenges with a positive and resilient mindset.

OK, enough with the metaphors, Bethany. How do we apply this wizardry? Begin any endeavor by setting clear and specific goals. These objectives serve as your guiding stars, keeping you on track and ensuring that every action is purposeful and aligned with your vision. Before embarking on a project, gather all the necessary information and resources. This could involve thorough research, the accumulation of relevant data, or the acquisition of tools and equipment essential to your undertaking. Create a comprehensive plan of action that outlines every step required to achieve your goals. A well-structured plan keeps you organized and focused, eliminating the chaos that can often derail progress. To sharpen your skills and refine your techniques, practice diligently before launching into any project. This rehearsal phase not only builds expertise but also identifies areas where improvement is needed.

While meticulous preparation is essential, it's equally vital to remain adaptable. Be prepared to adjust your plan as unexpected challenges arise. Flexibility ensures you can navigate detours and continue moving forward. And you can only do this if you actually put all this preparation into actual action. Learn. Prepare. Then DO. Please do not take from this entire book that you must remain in the preparation phase until you or your plan are perfect. There is no perfect. Learn. Prepare. Then DO. Then learn some more. Adapt. Then DO some more. And if I have done my job well, you will do the doing from your lane, whilst your OPs enjoy doing from theirs.

Let's illustrate the power of preparation with a few real-life examples:

- **Launching a New Product:** Before introducing a new product to the market, invest time in researching your target audience. Gather feedback from potential customers to fine-tune your offering, ensuring it aligns with their needs and desires. Then trust that and LAUNCH.
- **Commencing a New Project:** For any project, gather the requisite tools and resources beforehand. Practice the necessary skills and techniques so you have more clarity when it's time to execute. Then EXECUTE.
- **Entering a New Market:** Expanding into a new market demands comprehensive research. Understand the competitive landscape, identify potential risks, and seize opportunities that lie ahead. Then GO.

- **Making Critical Business Decisions:** Before making major business decisions, seek counsel and advice from trusted OPs. Their insights can provide invaluable guidance in ensuring informed and well-rounded choices. Then DECIDE.

In essence, Abraham Lincoln's wisdom reminds us that success is driven just as much by smart work as it is by hard work. By taking the time to sharpen your axe through thorough preparation, you become equipped to tackle any challenge with confidence and finesse. Preparation is your all-powerful tool that ensures every effort is purposeful, efficient, and, ultimately, successful. Measure twice and cut once, and let the art of preparation guide you towards the realization of your dreams and the creation of a magical life. And then get to work.

Celebrate Your Wins: The Power of Bragging

Do you find yourself downplaying your successes or hesitating to share your accomplishments with others? It's time to rethink that approach. Bragging can actually be good for your business. It's true. I told you earlier we brag here, so let's discuss it.

Celebrating your wins is well established as a healthy practice. It boosts morale and motivation, both for you and for your team. Recognizing and celebrating achievements reinforces the value of hard work and encourages continued effort towards future successes. Additionally, celebrating your wins can help build your brand and reputation. Sharing your accomplishments with others helps to establish your credibility, showcase your strengths and expertise, and can lead to new opportunities for growth and expansion.

While the term bragging may have negative connotations, it's important to recognize that there's a difference between healthy self-promotion and arrogant boasting. By sharing your successes with others, you're not only celebrating your achievements but also building your personal and professional brand. Bragging can help establish you as an authority in your field, attract new clients or customers, and even create new business opportunities. Allow yourself to be the thought-leading badass you are. If no one knows about it, what's the point? Tree falling in the forest kind of thing. So don't be afraid to brag a little—celebrate your wins and let the world know about your accomplishments. In fact, be afraid not to. Well, maybe not afraid. Just brag.

The Neuroscience of Bragging

Bragging may seem like an act of vanity or arrogance, but the truth is, it's actually rooted in science. Neuroscience supports bragging. More science from a lawyer? Awesome. But I like facts supported by data.

The act of bragging activates the brain's reward center, triggering the release of dopamine, a neurotransmitter associated with pleasure and motivation. This surge of dopamine creates feelings of happiness and satisfaction, which in turn reinforces the behavior of bragging. This is a positive feedback loop that brings that exponential growth I've been harping on about.

Sharing positive experiences and accomplishments with others activates the brain's mirror neurons, which are responsible for empathy and social bonding. When you share your successes with others, they will feel a sense of pride and excitement for you, leading to increased social connection and trust. This is exactly why I am always in a mastermind group in addition to my private coaching. Success is contagious. And it actually loves company, so let's replace misery with bragging.

While bragging can have many benefits, it's important to do it effectively and without coming across as arrogant or self-centered.

You've all seen *that* guy. You know the one. You see his videos and cringe. Don't be a douche about it. The best way to do that is to be authentic. Share your successes in a genuine and honest way. If you're really, truly being your authentic self, then screw anyone who calls you douchey. It's a lot easier to judge someone than to work your ass off to actually succeed. That said, avoid exaggerating or inflating your accomplishments—what you have accomplished is impressive enough. Own that.

In addition to focusing on what you did well, also point out the positive impact your success had on Others or your business. People want to know how what you created benefitted Others and can benefit them. When you've applied the concepts in this book, then you got to where you are with a lot of Other People helping you out, so it's important to recognize the contributions of your OPs.

One final thought on bragging: If you are spending most of your time with winners, most of what lower-case other people would consider bragging is just sharing your wins with each other. Winners will help each other up their game, even when it comes to bragging. Always choose your Other People wisely.

The Joy of Scalable Success: Building a Business That's Also Fun!

So often, people focus only on the lofty goals of financial success, growth, and impact. While these objectives are undoubtedly crucial, there's another facet of building a business that deserves equal attention—the element of FUN! Social media and many gurus often portray entrepreneurship as a relentless grind, characterized by long hours, sleepless nights, and unending stress. It is all of those things for sure. But I wholeheartedly believe it is essential to debunk the myth that success must come at the expense of happiness and enjoyment. We can bust our asses, build our empires, *and* we can enjoy the shit out of it without diminishing our accomplishments.

To infuse fun into your business and wealth creation, start by redefining what success means to you. I hope you already did that at the beginning of the book. If you didn't, take a moment to reflect on it now. Instead of solely measuring it in financial terms or market dominance, consider success as a blend of personal fulfillment, impact on others, and the sheer joy of the whole trip. When you align your definition of success with your passion and values, the process becomes inherently enjoyable. Let me be clear: I am not saying it will always be fun and I am not saying it will always be easy. I am saying that you can and should do the things that bring you the most joy while driving you closer to your goals as often as you can. Refer to your Absofuckinglutely Analyzer as needed.

One key to having fun in business is pursuing opportunities that align with your passions and interests. When you're genuinely enthusiastic about what you do, it's no longer just work; it becomes a source of inspiration and delight. Passion fuels creativity and innovation, making your work both engaging and enjoyable. Add to that passion a healthy dose of solving OP problems, and you might just have yourself a self-sustaining, self-perpetuating business.

Of course, running a business can feel overwhelming when you try to do everything yourself. Embracing the principle of Other People's Everything, delegate tasks and responsibilities to those who excel in those areas. This not only lightens your workload but also allows you to focus on what you're passionate about, making your work more enjoyable.

The culture you create within your organization plays a significant role in making your business fun. Foster an environment where creativity, collaboration, and a sense of purpose thrive. Celebrate achievements (read: brag more), encourage open communication, and prioritize work-life balance. A positive culture can turn the workplace into a source of joy for you and your team.

Continuous learning and personal growth are intrinsically rewarding. Challenge yourself to acquire new skills, explore uncharted territories, and expand your horizons. The excitement of learning and self-improvement can infuse your entrepreneurial journey with a sense of adventure and enthusiasm.

Amidst the daily grind of business, take the time to acknowledge what you have accomplished so far. Whether it's reaching a financial milestone, launching a successful product, or achieving a personal goal, acknowledging your accomplishments reminds you of your progress and brings joy to the process. See *The Gap and The Gain* by Dr. Benjamin Hardy and Dan Sullivan for more on appreciating how far you've come versus judging how far you have yet to go.

Maintaining a balance between work and play is essential. Schedule regular breaks, vacations, and moments of leisure to recharge your energy and creativity. Remember that downtime is not a distraction from success but a crucial component of it. I know we are all working to build a life we don't need a vacation from. I get it. But we often have our most brilliant insights when we take a step back from the work and the business. In fact, I was speaking with a client of mine, a super successful real estate investor and community builder, Brandon Turner, at a retreat we both attended, and he said he gets his best million-dollar ideas when he's getting his regular massages. Guess who has two thumbs and now gets regular massages? This woman right here. And I'm here to tell you, the benefits are more than just a relaxing moment away. The clarity and creativity that flood you when you are in a deep state of relaxation are worth the time and money.

Plus, going on adventures and creating memories with the people you love make you happier, more interesting, and more successful. Look at Richard Branson. He's arguably the most successful person in the world, and he is always playing and creating and having fun, even when he's working. And before you grumble that it's easy for a billionaire to go on adventures and make everything into play, I will let you in on a little secret: That is precisely *how* he was able to become a billionaire. So, quit grumbling and go outside and play!

The pursuit of success need not be a solemn, joyless endeavor. By infusing your business with passion, purpose, and a commitment to personal fulfillment, you can create a scalable venture that's also FUN! As you embrace the principles of OPE, remember that building a business that brings you joy not only enriches your life but also inspires others to pursue their dreams with a sense of enthusiasm and purpose. Another tried and true saying comin' at ya: "In the end, it's not just about the destination; it's about the joy ride."

Conclusion

Ryan Elsey, a private equity fund manager and retired law enforcement professional, said, "One of the strings attached to all the blessings we enjoy is the responsibility to share them with others." As business owners and professionals, we have the opportunity to enjoy a variety of blessings, including financial success, career achievements, and personal fulfillment. However, with these blessings comes a responsibility to share them with Others and give back to our communities.

This reminds us that success is not just about achieving our own goals and ambitions but also about making a positive impact on the world around us. So, how can we live up to this responsibility and share our blessings with Others?

One of the most powerful ways to share your blessings is to give back to your community. This can include volunteering your time, donating to local charities, or supporting local businesses and organizations. As a successful business owner or professional, you have a wealth of knowledge and experience to share with others. Consider mentoring young professionals, students, or aspiring entrepreneurs to help them achieve their own goals and reach their full potential. Consider using your business or personal resources to support social and environmental causes that align with your values. This can include supporting organizations that promote sustainability, social justice, or human rights.

One of the most important ways to share your blessings is to run your business ethically and responsibly. This means treating your employees, customers, and suppliers with respect and fairness and conducting your business in a way that promotes sustainability and social responsibility. Finally, remember your actions speak louder than words. By living your values and sharing your blessings with Others, you can be a role model for Others to follow.

Keep in mind that your journey toward conscious wealth, empire-building, and a magical life is an ongoing process. Continuously seek out new opportunities, expand your network, and adapt to the changing landscape of your goals and aspirations. The power of OPE is boundless, and its potential to transform your life is limited only by your willingness to explore, connect, and take action. With each step you take, each Other Person you collaborate with, and each system you implement, you are one step closer to realizing your vision of a magical life.

Your magical life is within reach. By embracing the concepts and strategies outlined in this book, you have the tools to leverage the power of OPE to its fullest extent. Belief, in this instance, is critical to the reality. It's not like flat Earthers and normal people debating whether the Earth is round. It doesn't matter what any of them believe. The Earth is just round. But when it comes to your ability to achieve your dreams and your magical life, you have to believe it before it can be true.

Appendix

506 (B)	506 (C)
• Unlimited Raise • Up to 35 Non-Accredited Investors Allowed • No Advertising • No General Solicitation • In General, Need a Preexisting Relationship With Prospective Investor • No Bad Actors Allowed as Syndicators or 20% Voting • Pre-Emptis State Law • Check The Box Verification OK	• Unlimited Raise • Accredited Investors Only • Advertising Allowed • General Solicitation Allowed • No Pre-Existing Relationships With Prospective Investor Needed • No Bad Actors as Syndicators or 20% Voting • Pre-Emptis State Law • Take Reasonable Steps to Verify Investors

THANK YOU FOR READING MY BOOK!

Just to say thanks for buying and reading my book,
I would like to give you a *free* gift, no strings attached!

SCAN ME

*I appreciate your interest in my book and
value your feedback as it helps me improve future
versions of this book. I would appreciate it
if you could leave your invaluable review on
Amazon.com with your feedback.
Thank you!*

www.ingramcontent.com/pod-product-compliance
Lightning Source LLC
Chambersburg PA
CBHW070702190326
41458CB00046B/6815/J